Disability *tax* Fairness

Report of the
Technical Advisory
Committee on
Tax Measures for
Persons with
Disabilities

*The views and recommendations put forward in this report are those of the
Technical Advisory Committee on Tax Measures for Persons with Disabilities
and do not necessarily reflect the views of the Department of Finance or
the Canada Revenue Agency.*

December 2004

The Honourable Ralph Goodale, P.C., M.P.
Minister of Finance
21st Floor, East Tower, L'Esplanade Laurier
140 O'Connor Street
Ottawa, Ontario K1A 0G5

The Honourable John McCallum, P.C., M.P.
Minister of National Revenue
4th Floor, Connaught Building
555 MacKenzie Avenue
Ottawa, Ontario K1A 0L5

Dear Ministers:

We are pleased to submit to you the report of the Technical Advisory Committee on Tax Measures for Persons with Disabilities.

The report was prepared by the Committee following extensive discussion and debate, which was aided by the research and expertise of individual Committee members. As such, all of the Committee support the broad conclusions and recommendations of the report.

We hope the report serves as a useful guide to the Government of Canada in improving the fairness of the treatment of persons with disabilities under the income tax system.

Respectfully submitted,

Sherri Torjman
Co-Chair

Robert D. Brown
Co-Chair

Brian J. Arnold

Michael Bach

Laurie Beachell

Harry Beatty

Gail Beck, M.D., C.M., F.R.C.P.C.

Gary Birch

Lembi Buchanan

Karen R. Cohen, Ph.D., C. Psych.

Yude M. Henteleff, C.M., Q.C.

Guy Lord

Table of Contents

Chapter 3: Employment- and Education-Related Tax Measures

Chapter 4: Measures for Caregivers and Children with Disabilities

Executive Summary

Executive Summary

Our Mandate

The Technical Advisory Committee on Tax Measures for Persons with Disabilities was announced in the 2003 federal budget to advise the Ministers of Finance and National Revenue on disability-related tax measures. The Committee was appointed in April 2003 and is composed of members of organizations representing persons with disabilities, health practitioners, and human rights and tax experts (see Appendix 1). In our deliberations, the members of the Committee worked together to address the issues referred to us, using our best personal judgments and experiences. We did not seek to represent the views of the various organizations with which we are associated.

The Committee's mandate was to make recommendations that would help the federal government improve the fairness of the treatment of persons with disabilities under the income tax system, taking into account available fiscal resources. We viewed fairness as requiring equitable treatment among persons with disabilities and between persons with disabilities with taxable income and without taxable income.

As an independent committee, we were able to determine the issues we wished to examine that related to our terms of reference, almost all of which were referred to in submissions from the disability community. While we attempted to address the breadth of concerns raised in the submissions in our deliberations and in our report, it was not possible to cover all the related issues. In fulfilling our mandate, we examined these issues within the context of the total range of supports and programs for persons with disabilities.

Our Process

The Committee actively sought the views of individuals and groups, and welcomed input from all interested parties. Early in our deliberations, we decided not to hold formal public hearings. We chose this route because organizations in the disability community typically face significant time and resource constraints, and recently had been consulted by the federal government on issues related to the disability tax credit, in particular.

We decided instead to build on the extensive consultations previously carried out by various departments, task forces and committees. More specifically, we referred to the work of the Sub-Committee of the House of Commons Standing Committee on Human Resources Development and the Status of Persons with Disabilities, which had embarked in 2001 upon a review of concerns regarding the disability tax credit. The Sub-Committee received submissions from major national disability and professional organizations. The first step in our process was to request permission from the Sub-Committee to obtain and publicly post these submissions to our website (www.disabilitytax.ca). We had created this website in order to share information and ensure the transparency of our work as well as provide a record of the input we received.

We then wrote to these same organizations, indicating our intent to make use of their earlier submissions and representations to the parliamentary Sub-Committee, and asked if they wished to update or add to these previous representations.

In addition to building upon this substantial base, we placed an ad in *Abilities* magazine and sent letters to approximately 400 disability groups and associations of relevant professionals. We invited them to make any submissions they might wish to the Committee and, in so doing, we encouraged them to examine the submissions already posted to our website. We welcomed additional representations that they might want to bring to our attention.

We felt that this process would reduce the burden on disability organizations while still providing them full opportunity to communicate their concerns and issues to our Committee. In response to our letter, we received a further 31 submissions over the course of our mandate for a total of 49 submissions. All submissions, other than representations on personal issues that we deemed confidential, were posted to our website while the Committee's work was under way. A list of organizations and individuals who made submissions to the Committee is attached as Appendix 2.

To supplement the issues identified by various organizations, the Committee commissioned several research papers and met with selected experts. This work is described in Appendix 3. In addition to the submissions and background papers, the Committee reviewed the extensive legacy of government reports on disability that have been written since 1981, the International Year of Disabled Persons. Committee members carried out extensive research and prepared numerous reports for discussion purposes.

Given the range and intricacies of tax measures, our review required considerable time and effort. The issues are complex, and we spent many hours and months debating the current measures and possible reforms. In the course of our deliberations, we received substantial data and assistance from officials of the Department of Finance and the

Canada Revenue Agency. But the conclusions are entirely our own; our contribution is to provide an independent view of the matters that we considered.

In arriving at our decisions, we were conscious of the two main aspects of our mandate: to improve tax fairness for persons with disabilities and to do so taking into account available fiscal resources.[1] We interpreted this mandate as follows.

First, we considered a wide range of possible actions and then developed a set of recommendations for improving the fairness of the tax system from both policy and administrative perspectives. We believe that the changes we are proposing represent significant improvements to the current system. They are important measures in themselves, even though we feel that, in future, additional funding for persons with disabilities should be directed through expenditure programs. We make a recommendation to this effect in the final chapter of the report.

We then prioritized our recommendations. The Committee recognizes that additional actions can be taken both to improve tax fairness and to expand the system of disability programs. But we also acknowledge that choices must be made among a wide range of potentially valuable investments. We therefore spent considerable time debating these options in order to provide guidance to the government as to our own preferences and priorities with respect to these choices.

Our recommendations focus explicitly upon the changes that can be made within the existing tax system to improve both the fairness and adequacy of several key provisions. We follow these recommendations with some reflections on the limitations of the tax system in addressing disability concerns within the context of the total support that society provides to persons with disabilities. We make some observations that may contribute to future progress in this broader area.

Our Proposals

The legacy of work on disability that has been undertaken in Canada articulates some key principles that influenced our own thinking. The 1996 Federal Task Force on Disability Issues chaired by the Honourable Andy Scott, for example, identified the following assumptions that guided its work around disability costs, in particular.[2] We were reminded of these in submissions to the parliamentary Sub-Committee from several groups, including the Council of Canadians with Disabilities.

- For persons with disabilities normal activities bring extraordinary costs that are involuntary.

---

[1] In the 2003 federal budget, the government set aside $25 million in 2003–04 and $80 million per year starting in 2004–05 to improve tax fairness for persons with disabilities, based on our recommendations and on its own evaluation of the disability tax credit. The 2004 federal budget reprofiled the $25 million set aside for 2003–04 to future years, so that the annual amount set aside was adjusted to $85 million per year.

[2] Federal Task Force on Disability Issues, *Equal Citizenship for Canadians with Disabilities: The will to act*, 1996, p. 87.

- Some of these costs are general and intangible and others can be supported by receipts for expenditures.
- Tax recognition of these costs is not a subsidy based on sympathy or charity but fair tax treatment.
- Tax recognition of disability-related costs should encourage, not discourage, the employment of persons with disabilities.
- The costs associated with disability are more onerous when borne by individuals with limited income.
- The costs associated with disability are not limited to those with taxable income.

In addition to these assumptions, our work was shaped by the following objectives. We sought to achieve fairness in the treatment of persons with different disabilities. We looked for solutions that would support independence and self-sufficiency in terms of education, employment and community participation. We recognized the importance of providing assistance to caregivers of children with severe disabilities. We were concerned with assisting those deemed to be most in need.

Our 24 recommendations for the reform of disability tax measures fall into three major themes, focused on achieving a fairer and more responsive tax system. First, there is a package of proposed changes to clarify the legislative and interpretive intent of the disability tax credit and to improve its administration. The second group of proposals focuses primarily upon the itemizable costs of disability and, more specifically, upon various tax measures that enable persons with disabilities to pursue education, training or employment. The third group of recommendations is intended to improve tax measures that recognize the additional costs of caregiving.

The first theme within the package proposes changes to the disability tax credit – the primary tax measure concerned with the non-itemizable or hidden costs of disability. Our proposals regarding the disability tax credit call for legislative, interpretive and administrative changes that reflect the principle of fairness.

These proposals seek to respond to the recommendations in the March 2002 report of the House of Commons Standing Committee on Human Resources Development and the Status of Persons with Disabilities, *Getting it Right for Canadians: The Disability Tax Credit*. The report called for changes to the eligibility requirements of the disability tax credit so as to clarify and broaden eligibility for the credit, make more fair the administration and appeals processes, and ensure that there is greater knowledge of and access to the measure.

More specifically, in order to improve the fairness of the disability tax credit, we recommend that individuals with multiple restrictions in activity that have a substantial overall impact on their everyday lives be eligible for the credit. We also call for further improvements in the administration of the disability tax credit, with the full participation of the disability community.

Our recommendations seek to achieve a 'full equality standard' for the disability tax credit. The policies and practices regarding the credit must ensure that all Canadians with disabilities are treated with *fairness*, and these policies and practices must be seen as *humane and compassionate*. Our proposals seek to *remove systemic barriers* to individuals who are already vulnerable not only financially but also psychologically.

With respect to education and employment measures, the Committee explored several options for enhancing existing, and creating new, incentives to work. In January 2004, we recommended the introduction of the disability supports deduction, which subsequently was announced in the 2004 federal budget. The new measure provides a deduction, rather than a limited credit, for certain costs incurred to enable persons with disabilities to participate in the labour force or attend school. This measure is described in more detail in the chapter on employment- and education-related measures.

The Committee then worked to propose enhancements to the new provision in order to expand the list of items that may be claimed for employment and educational purposes. The deduction also addresses the taxation of government assistance of disability supports. We strongly suggest that the government take immediate steps to rectify the situation if, in future, it finds instances of this assistance being subject to tax.

The Committee calls for an increase to the refundable medical expense supplement that would provide additional assistance to low-income working Canadians who incur very high disability-related costs. We also recommend changes to registered education savings plans to accommodate the diverse needs of persons with disabilities.

The disability supports deduction and associated enhancements are directed toward individual taxpayers. We recommend that the government review, as part of its efforts to encourage the full participation of persons with disabilities, a tax measure used in the United States to encourage employers to hire persons with disabilities and other groups with high unemployment rates.

The third cluster of proposals focuses upon the tax measures that provide some recognition of the costs that caregivers incur in providing support for adults with disabilities and that families sustain in raising children with disabilities. For direct costs, we recommend a doubling of the limit of medical expenses that caregivers may claim in respect of a dependant with a severe disability. We also propose an increase to the Child Disability Benefit paid to the parents of children who are eligible for the disability tax credit.

Finally, we recommend that the government examine ways to allow greater flexibility as to how the private savings of a caregiver can be used to provide ongoing support to a dependent child or grandchild with a disability in the event of the caregiver's death. This measure will help these families to ensure a better quality of life for their children or grandchildren with severe disabilities.

All the recommendations put forward by the Committee were made within the context of the current tax system. Taken together, the proposed changes represent limited, but important, steps toward promoting the equality rights of persons with disabilities and encouraging their participation in the workforce and society. The suggested measures will better reflect the ability to pay income tax by recognizing the direct and hidden costs of disability. We believe that the long-term effects of the changes we propose will improve the quality of life of persons with disabilities and their families by enhancing their independence and self-sufficiency.

We also note throughout the report a number of possible measures that warrant future consideration and study. These include the potential for expanded use of a social model of disability for disability-related measures. We also support a move towards the full deductibility of all disability-related support costs. Other noteworthy initiatives could include the simplification of tax provisions for caregivers, the introduction of measures to encourage savings by family members to assist persons with disabilities and the extension of the Child Disability Benefit to middle-income families.

The estimated total annual ongoing cost of our recommendations amounts to $110 million in direct tax relief to persons with disabilities, plus $2 million in administrative costs (see Table). While we recognize that our proposals modestly exceed the government's allocation of $85 million, we believe that all of our recommendations represent important steps to improve tax fairness for persons with disabilities.

The recommendations outlined below are only those with cost implications. Our full list of recommendations is attached at the end of this report.

While we have made a total of 24 recommendations for improving current tax measures, we acknowledge that the concerns and needs of persons with disabilities go well beyond the specific provisions we were asked to explore. Many of the remedies that have been proposed over the years are found in mechanisms that lie outside of the tax system. We suggest that as additional resources become available they should be directed to non-tax measures. We share some of our thoughts on these related issues in our final chapter, Future Directions.

Summary of Recommendations with a Fiscal Cost

Legislative and Interpretive Recommendations	Estimated Annual Ongoing Cost[1,2] ($ millions)
Disability Tax Credit	
1. Changing the eligibility criteria	
Recommendation 2.4	50
Employment- and Education-Related Tax Measures	
1. Introducing a disability supports deduction	
Recommendation 3.1	15[3]
2. Expanding the disability supports deduction	
Recommendation 3.2	5
3. Enhancing the refundable medical expense supplement	
Recommendation 3.5	20
4. Changing registered education savings plans	
Recommendation 3.6	s[4]
Measures for Caregivers and Children with Disabilities	
1. Increasing the limit of expenses claimable by caregivers under the medical expense tax credit	
Recommendation 4.1	5
2. Changing the rules regarding rollovers of proceeds from registered retirement savings plans (RRSPs) and registered retirement income funds (RRIFs)	
Recommendation 4.2	s[4]
3. Increasing the Child Disability Benefit	
Recommendation 4.3	15
Total of legislative and interpretive recommendations	**110**
Administrative Recommendations	
Disability Tax Credit	
1. Implementing administrative changes	
Recommendations 2.7, 2.11[5]	2
Total	**112**

---

[1] All cost estimates were provided by the Department of Finance or the Canada Revenue Agency.

[2] Cost estimates assume full implementation in 2004–05. Ongoing costs for some measures will increase over time.

[3] This measure was announced in the 2004 federal budget.

[4] Small: less than $5 million.

[5] Recommendation 2.11 (investigation of alternative dispute resolution process) does not have a recognized ongoing cost in this table because it cannot be determined at this time, but the recommended pilot project is estimated to cost $4 million over one to two years.

Chapter 1:
The Context

Chapter 1: The Context

The mandate of the Committee was to explore the role, effectiveness and fairness of disability-related tax measures. While this mandate was very specific, we knew that it would be necessary to place our work within the context of broader debates around disability that have taken place over the past few decades across the country and, indeed, throughout the world.

These debates have focused upon the recognition of persons with disabilities as citizens of equal worth and entitlement. Ensuring their fullest participation enables them to make a positive social and economic contribution – a benefit both to the individuals and to society.

The Committee was also influenced by the extensive legacy of reports on disability that have been written since 1981, the International Year of Disabled Persons. This year is often cited as a landmark or turning point at which time governments around the world began to pay attention to disability issues. We tried to ensure that our work was consistent with the evolution over a near quarter-century of the knowledge and attitudes in this area.

Citizenship Perspective on Disability

Inclusion

Citizenship is often understood as an ability to participate and be included in all aspects of society. Canadian governments have recognized repeatedly the importance of participation and inclusion for persons with disabilities, beginning in the early 1990s, when the federal, provincial and territorial governments issued *Mainstream 1992: Pathway to Integration*. This work was intended to ensure that persons with disabilities have access to all public programs and to the same goods and services as other Canadians.

Inclusion was identified as an overarching national goal by the federal-provincial-territorial document *In Unison: A Canadian Approach to Disability Issues*, which sought ways to guarantee that persons with disabilities could participate in virtually all aspects of community life. Our proposals are consistent with this vision.

The Committee's recommendations seek to make the tax system fairer for persons with disabilities, promote greater equity among various sectors of the disability community and ensure that the tax system recognizes that Canadians with disabilities face substantive disadvantage. But while our recommendations for improved tax fairness are significant, we acknowledge that they are only small steps to enhance access to disability supports and to educational and employment opportunities. Nor do they address in any substantive way the poverty experienced by many Canadians with disabilities.

Accommodation

The federal government again affirmed its commitment to full participation in its 2002 report, *Advancing the Inclusion of Persons with Disabilities*. One way to promote inclusion is through accommodation, which basically means finding ways to make certain that persons with disabilities can maximize their participation in any given program, event, opportunity or environment. The intervention may be as small as modifying a door handle or as substantial as redesigning a work process.

Accommodation can be achieved through the provision of a disability support, such as technical aid, special equipment or personal assistance, which enables an individual to carry out an activity of daily living to the fullest of his or her capacity. Families, caregivers and employers play important roles in providing this assistance.

Modifications to the physical environment to remove barriers, such as installation of ramps or rearrangement of internal spaces and furniture, are other significant measures. Barrier-free design generally is considered the starting point for accommodation. This type of design is helpful not only for persons with disabilities. It makes the world more manageable for everyone. Curb cuts, for example, are easier for young children, the elderly, parents with baby strollers and persons with mobility impairments. Clear language and large print improve clarity for all, including persons with learning, visual or intellectual disabilities.

But accommodation involves more than physical adaptation. Individual needs often can be accommodated through adjustment of a rule, requirement or procedure. A person with a severe learning disability, for example, may need additional time to complete a school assignment or exam, or may even require a modified course load or curriculum. Someone with chronic fatigue syndrome or multiple sclerosis may be able to continue working with a flexible schedule.

Regardless of the form of accommodation, it effectively seeks to encourage a sharing of the additional costs of disability. The accommodation of disability-related needs within any setting – child care centres, schools, post-secondary educational institutions and workplaces – often reduces the amount that individuals themselves must pay for additional assistance or customization. The costs of accommodation effectively are built into the space, facility or program.

It has been almost 10 years since the Federal Task Force on Disability Issues noted the importance of accommodation:

> The federal government should concern itself with ways to minimize or eliminate additional disadvantages of costs and lack of mobility that Canadian citizens face because they have disabilities.
>
> This means that every government program should, as a matter of principle, incorporate the individual and particular needs of persons with disabilities in the very core of its design. A good example of what we mean is the Canada Student Loans Program. Certain criteria such as the number of courses a student can take, or the length of time to complete a program, are flexible so that all eligible students with disabilities can qualify for a loan.
>
> At the same time, we recognize that the additional costs of disadvantages that result from disabilities cannot always be accommodated in each and every 'mainstream' program. Where this is the case, a complementary measure, designed to mesh with the generic program can be put in place to ensure that no one is denied the opportunity to participate just because of disability.[1]

Accommodation is important because it helps reduce individual financial burden by sharing the costs of disability. When persons with disabilities are able to participate fully in education, training and employment, they become contributing members of society. Many pay income tax and 'return' the accommodation investments made on their behalf. When persons with disabilities are able to participate in all aspects of society, they can enjoy the full rights and responsibilities of citizenship.

Our examination of the various disability tax measures ultimately led to debates about the role of these tax provisions relative to the overarching national goals of citizenship and inclusion. Our immediate concerns focused upon the principle of equity and how the tax measures we were asked to consider could be made fairer and more equitable. As we explored the role of tax provisions relative to the broader goals of citizenship and inclusion, and the immediate goals of equity and fairness, we found ourselves grappling with a number of difficult questions.

First, how should disability be defined? This question was particularly relevant to our discussions of the disability tax credit. But it is important for other tax measures as well as for programs and services. In answering this question, we turned to the social model, which takes into account how well society accommodates impairment in function.

Second, in acknowledging that persons with disabilities incur additional costs, what is the role of the tax system with respect to these costs? Our recommendations represent our attempt to answer this question.

---

[1] Federal Task Force on Disability Issues, *Equal Citizenship for Canadians with Disabilities: The will to act*, 1996, p. 12.

Finally, is the tax system the most appropriate delivery mechanism for recognizing disability-related costs? We explore this last question in the final chapter, Future Directions.

Defining Disability

Any measure that provides assistance to persons with disabilities – whether a program, service, income support or tax relief – quickly runs into a common problem. The question arises as to how to define disability in order to determine eligibility.

At the current time, a wide range of definitions is used to determine eligibility for various programs and tax measures. The issues arising from multiple eligibility criteria were documented in a recent federal report entitled *Defining Disability: A Complex Issue.*[2]

The term 'disability' captures diverse conditions and causal factors. There are many different types of disability related to mobility, hearing, seeing, mental function, learning and development. And there are varying degrees of severity and impairment within and across types of disability. While tax measures and other disability supports require that lines be drawn for eligibility purposes, all such lines are arbitrary to some extent. Inevitably, the difference between those who qualify and those who do not is often small.

Data from the 2001 Participation and Activity Limitation Survey conducted by Statistics Canada indicate that an estimated 3.6 million Canadians – or 12 percent of the population – experienced some limitations in their everyday activities because of physical, psychological or health conditions.[3] Data from the 2000–01 Canadian Community Health Survey show that the rate of disability is significantly higher among Aboriginal Canadians, 31 percent of whom reported having a disability.[4] The limits of the tax system in addressing the needs of Aboriginal Canadians are discussed in Chapter 5.

Not surprisingly, the rate of disability rises with age. About 3 percent of children up to age 14 have a disability compared with 53 percent of seniors age 75 and over.

Looking only at the adult population, the Participation and Activity Limitation Survey reported that an estimated 3.4 million adult Canadians – or 15 percent of the adult population – had some form of disability in 2001. Of this total, the survey revealed that about 1.2 million persons had a mild degree of activity limitation and 860,000 had a

---

[2] Government of Canada, *Defining Disability: A Complex Issue*, 2003.

[3] Human Resources Development Canada, *Disability in Canada: A 2001 Profile*, 2003, pp. 2, 46, 51.

[4] The Canadian Community Health Survey data do not include information on Aboriginal people living on First Nations reserves and are not directly comparable to the data from the Participation and Activity Limitation Survey. For more information, see Government of Canada, *Advancing the Inclusion of Persons with Disabilities*, 2002, pp. 6–7.

moderate degree of activity limitation.[5] Approximately 920,000 and 480,000 Canadians are reported to have severe and very severe levels, respectively, of activity limitation.[6]

While these statistics provide a general overview of the incidence of disability in Canada, there is a great deal of variation within the population of persons with disabilities. Some people are born with disabling conditions such as spina bifida. Others acquire a disability, such as multiple sclerosis, in the course of their lifetime. Still others may become disabled as a result of an accident, as in the case of a worker who loses a limb at a factory or a person who becomes paralyzed because of a motor vehicle or sports-related accident. Many individuals experience impairment in function due to the effects of aging; vascular dementia is just one example.

The Committee also learned in the course of our work that the conceptualization of disability has been changing over time. Disability used to be understood in fairly narrow terms. The mere presence of certain conditions used to mean that a person was disabled. This approach, referred to as the 'medical model,' typically views disability as a health problem or personal abnormality.

The influence of the medical model became especially apparent in our discussions of the disability tax credit, which in its application to date has had serious difficulties with the recognition of mental disabilities. Because the effects are often not immediately obvious or easily measurable, persons with mental disabilities frequently are not identified as having a disability even though they may be more restricted in function than some persons with physical disabilities.

We learned that the emerging social model, by contrast, views disability largely as a problem of how well (or not) society accommodates impairment in function. When environments are adapted to individual need, the effects of a disability can be reduced in severity.

The proposition that disability should be understood as the effects of impairment within a given context is consistent with work under way throughout the world.

In 2001, for example, the World Health Organization released the latest version of the International Classification of Functioning, Disability and Health, in which disability was seen to arise from the interaction between impairments and externally imposed limitations on activity. The federal government has also acknowledged the evolution of thinking in this area:

---

[5] Human Resources Development Canada, *Disability in Canada: A 2001 Profile*, 2003, p. 53.

[6] The Statistics Canada survey is based on self-evaluation, and its results are not necessarily consistent with other measures that derive from independent health and activity evaluations.

For many decades, disability was seen as a set of characteristics of the individual –
a person *was* disabled or *had* a disability [italics in original]. As such, governments'
and society's interventions involved protecting the individual and the community,
or treating and fixing the impairment. But in the past two decades, as the disability
rights movement has emerged, the concept of disability has shifted from individual
impairment to a more social phenomenon. In this social view, persons with disabilities
are seen as being restricted in performing daily activities because of a complex set
of interrelating factors, some pertaining to the person and some pertaining to the
person's immediate environment and social/political arrangements.[7]

The key feature of a social model of disability is the recognition that a disability does
not lie solely in the individual, in his or her genetic differences, disease, long-term health
condition, or impairment in physical, sensory or mental functioning. Disability is also
determined by the limitations in carrying out activities of daily living, and in participating
in the social, economic, political and cultural life of the community. These limitations
can derive from the condition or impairment itself, in the context of other individual
conditions and factors, from social attitudes toward such conditions and/or from ways of
designing and organizing social, economic and built environments.[8] Often the limitation
that arises from a particular condition can be significantly ameliorated if the social stereotypes,
need for supports and environmental barriers are adequately addressed. There are many
examples of how advances in technology and treatment have had a dramatic impact upon
the ability to carry out daily activities.

Advancing the inclusion of people with disabilities requires action at various levels,
including provision of needed supports to individuals; ensuring families and caregivers
have the supports they need to play their roles; enabling communities to remove the
physical and architectural barriers to access; ensuring that community services, schools
and workplaces provide full accommodation; and addressing long-standing negative
stereotypes about people with disabilities. Our discussions have been guided by this
understanding of disability, and by our effort to explore ways the tax system might
address the disabling effects of individuals' conditions and the environments in which
they live, learn and work.

Disability-Related Costs

While disabilities vary widely in their impact, they often give rise to a common problem.
Persons with disabilities are likely to incur additional costs and to require assistance in
order to participate actively in and contribute to society.

[7] Government of Canada, *Advancing the Inclusion of Persons with Disabilities*, 2002, pp. 10–11.

[8] Roeher Institute, *Moving In Unison into Action: Towards a Policy Strategy for Improving Access to Disability Supports*, 2002.

The Participation and Activity Limitation Survey found that in 2001 an estimated 1.6 million persons age 15 and over with disabilities (out of a total 3.4 million persons) required assistive aids and devices. While most of these individuals said that they were able to obtain all the needed aids and devices, a sizeable minority (approximately 40 percent) reported that they could not.[9] Among those with unmet needs for assistive aids, the high cost of the equipment was cited as the main reason, particularly for persons with severe or very severe disabilities.

Persons with disabilities also face further costs in terms of lost opportunities. Many experience a diminished capacity to earn income – they can work only a few hours or days a week, if at all. Many caregivers forego paid employment to stay home and care for their child or other relative with a disability. As a result, persons with disabilities and caregivers face higher rates of unemployment, which often leads to lower incomes and higher rates of poverty.

Data from the Participation and Activity Limitation Survey indicated that about 40 percent of children with mild and moderate disabilities have family members whose employment is affected by the child's disability. The proportion rises to 73 percent among children whose disabilities are considered severe.[10] This foregone employment has an impact not only on current levels of income but also on the value of future pensions. Because mothers are usually the primary caregivers of children, it is their employment that is most often affected by their child's condition.

Disability Costs and the Tax System

The federal tax system has a number of measures that recognize the special circumstances of persons with disabilities. Within the tax system, the personal income tax system is the most direct way to reach Canadians with disabilities and has the most significant measures. Our focus is upon personal income tax measures, though we also touch briefly on the corporate tax system. A summary of the various personal income tax measures for persons with disabilities and for caregivers is provided in Appendix 4.

The personal income tax system has two key functions. The first and primary role is to raise revenue for the government. The second and more recent function is to act as a delivery vehicle for social programs – most notably income-tested benefits such as the Canada Child Tax Benefit.

As a revenue-raising mechanism, the personal income tax system must, and must be seen to, treat Canadians fairly. While there will always be debate about what makes a fair

---

[9] Human Resources Development Canada, *Disability in Canada: A 2001 Profile*, 2003, p. 60.

[10] Statistics Canada, *Children with disabilities and their families*, Catalogue no. 89-585-XIE, 2003, p. 9.

tax system, there is a generally accepted principle that income taxes should be levied according to ability to pay. The concept of tax fairness has two components.

The first is vertical equity, which suggests that those with higher incomes should pay more tax. In the Canadian tax system, vertical equity is achieved primarily through the progressive income tax rate structure.

The second dimension of fairness is horizontal equity, under which individuals with similar incomes in similar circumstances should pay similar amounts of tax. In practice, this principle involves providing tax credits or deductions to help recognize non-discretionary costs that reduce individuals' ability to pay tax relative to other taxpayers with the same total income. This recognition is not meant to subsidize or offset these costs, but rather to achieve equity and greater fairness in the allocation of the tax burden.

In the case of persons with disabilities, the principal measures that recognize additional costs are the disability tax credit, the medical expense tax credit and the disability supports deduction proposed in the 2004 federal budget. There are also cost recognition measures for family caregivers, notably the caregiver credit and the infirm dependant credit. Several other tax provisions available to all Canadians have special rules that take into account the circumstances of persons with disabilities.

There are various tax measures that recognize the impact of the costs of accommodation upon the ability to pay tax. The disability supports deduction, introduced in response to one of the Committee's recommendations, ensures that the cost of disability supports purchased for purposes of employment or education are fully deductible. The corporate tax system provides full deductibility of certain capital expenses incurred by businesses to accommodate the special needs of persons with disabilities, whether as customers or as employees.

As noted, the income tax system now delivers some income-tested benefits. For persons with disabilities and their families, there are two measures of interest. The first is the refundable medical expense supplement, which refunds to low-income workers a portion of the expenses recognized under the medical expense tax credit, and the disability supports deduction. The second is the Child Disability Benefit, which is delivered as a supplement to the Canada Child Tax Benefit to families caring for a child eligible for the disability tax credit.

We explore several of these measures in some detail, most notably the disability tax credit. We also discuss the taxability of disability-related income and support programs, and examine tax-assisted savings vehicles for families with children with severe disabilities.

The tax system generally recognizes out-of-pocket disability-related costs that can be identified and supported for tax purposes. These are often referred to as 'itemizable costs.' They include personal help with everyday living, technical aids and devices, and modifications to homes, vehicles and workplaces. These costs may be incurred by the person with a disability or by a supporting person. The medical expense tax credit and the disability supports deduction recognize many of these itemizable disability-related expenses.

At the same time, there are some disability-related expenses that may be more difficult to determine with precision. These non-itemizable costs of disability are not easily measured or quantified.

For example, some individuals may need to take a taxi to a locale that normally would be considered within walking distance. Others must purchase prepared food because they are unable to cook on their own. Many pay additional costs for specially altered clothing or may have to replace garments more frequently due to wear and tear from the use of assistive equipment or prosthetic appliances. Caregivers may also face higher costs – itemizable and non-itemizable – in respect of the support they provide for their children with disabilities.

Because non-itemizable costs cannot be readily measured, the tax system recognizes them through a flat amount that can be claimed by individuals who meet certain criteria. The disability tax credit is a prime example of this kind of measure.

The purpose of tax credits and deductions is to help determine what portion of income, if any, should be remitted to the government, rather than to compensate for lack of income or to reimburse individuals for their out-of-pocket costs. While our mandate called for us to examine disability-related tax measures, we felt that it was important to look at this particular delivery mechanism within the context of the total system of support for persons with disabilities.

Given both the federal nature of Canada's government and the vast differences in types and severity of disabilities, it is not surprising that this system is extraordinarily complex. Income assistance and disability supports are delivered by a wide variety of measures and programs. Families of persons with disabilities also provide substantial caregiving and other supports.

Employed-sponsored disability insurance is a major component of income support for many persons, but is not available to all persons with disabilities. Provinces and territories run the most important publicly provided disability-related programs.

These typically involve direct support to individuals through income assistance, provision of disability equipment and aids, and services at home.

Support sometimes is delivered through individual funding. Individuals receive a designated amount, according to their specific needs, to enable the purchase of required goods and services. The Canada Study Grant for Students with Permanent Disabilities, for example, helps offset the cost of supports required to participate in post-secondary education.

Programs vary by jurisdiction and by disability. Taken together, they provide a substantial amount of assistance but they are far from seamless or universally effective. Measures for persons with disabilities consist of a patchwork of programs and tax measures that are not fully integrated. These measures make available some appreciable level of support for some but less than adequate assistance for others. They comprise a bewildering maze that persons with disabilities face when seeking support.

In the final chapter of this report, we make some general comments about the overall system. For now, as we review the various tax measures that are the direct subject of our mandate, it is important to recognize that these represent only a modest part of the total picture. It is to these tax measures that we now turn.

Chapter 2:
Disability
Tax Credit

Chapter 2: Disability Tax Credit

Introduction

The disability tax credit provides tax relief to individuals with severe impairments in function that restrict them in activities of daily living. It is also available to some who require extensive therapy to sustain a vital function. The credit is based on the assumption that these individuals likely incur a range of disability-related costs that they are not able to claim under the medical expense tax credit, such as expenses associated with transportation and housing. These are considered to be the so-called non-itemizable or hidden costs of disability, as we described in the previous chapter.

The purpose of the disability tax credit is to provide for greater tax equity by allowing some relief for disability costs, since these are an unavoidable additional expense not faced by other taxpayers. In effect, the disability tax credit provides tax relief for assumed non-itemizable costs of $6,486 (the credit amount for 2004), which translates to a reduction of federal income tax otherwise owing or payable of a maximum of $1,038 (16 percent of $6,486).[1] The credit therefore is intended to act as a tax fairness measure rather than a subsidy or support for persons with disabilities.[2]

More specifically, the disability tax credit is designed to achieve a degree of horizontal equity in the tax system. According to the principle of horizontal equity, individuals in similar circumstances (i.e., having similar amounts of disposable income before tax) should pay similar amounts of tax. Appendix 5 illustrates how the disability tax credit seeks to achieve this objective.

The disability tax credit, however, is very much a blunt instrument. It grants a flat credit, regardless of the actual costs of disability, to individuals who meet the eligibility criteria, and hence may afford too little relief to some and too much to others. To some extent, this limitation is inherent in any broadly based tax measure designed to provide special tax treatment for persons with disabilities. There are serious limitations, as we will discuss in the Future Directions chapter, in the ability of the tax system to give fully equitable relief in response to the special circumstances faced by persons with severe disabilities.

Individuals who do not benefit from the disability tax credit because of insufficient federal tax liability (due primarily to low income), but who are eligible on the basis of disability, may transfer all or part of the credit to a supporting person. This supporting person includes a spouse or common-law partner, or a parent, grandparent, child,

---

[1] The disability tax credit, like other non-refundable credits, is calculated by multiplying a certain *amount* by a *credit rate*. The 16 percent credit rate is equivalent to the marginal tax rate on the first $35,000 of taxable income. The credit amount is indexed to the cost of living. In addition, provinces and territories generally grant a similar credit against provincial/territorial income tax, and the amount of tax relief from both federal and provincial/territorial disability tax credits averages approximately $1,600.

[2] Because the disability tax credit is primarily a fairness measure, it is not income tested and is available to all eligible taxpayers.

grandchild, brother, sister, aunt, uncle, nephew or niece of the individual.[3]
If the supporting person also has low income, that person may not benefit from
such a transfer.

Eligibility for the Disability Tax Credit

Who is Eligible for the Disability Tax Credit?

To be eligible for the disability tax credit, individuals must:
- have a *severe* and *prolonged* mental or physical *impairment*;

- as a result of that impairment, be *markedly restricted all or substantially all of the time* in their ability to perform a *basic activity of daily living*, or would be markedly restricted were it not for extensive therapy they receive to sustain a vital function; and

- file with the Canada Revenue Agency a form T2201, *Disability Tax Credit Certificate*, that has been completed by a qualified practitioner certifying that they meet the first two requirements.

For the purposes of the disability tax credit, 'prolonged' means that the impairment
has lasted or is expected to last for a continuous period of at least 12 months. 'Markedly
restricted' means that all or substantially all of the time, a person is blind or is unable,
or requires an inordinate amount of time, to perform a basic activity of daily living,
even with therapy and the use of appropriate devices and medication.

The Canada Revenue Agency informed us that it generally has interpreted the requirement
'all or substantially all of the time' to mean that the restrictions in activity are present
90 percent of the time or more. This interpretation is also applied to other sections
of the *Income Tax Act* that use the phrase 'all or substantially all of the time.' It should
be noted that the courts have indicated that a single mathematical test cannot be applied
to the phrase 'substantially all' and, therefore, the 90 percent interpretation serves merely
as a guideline.

In determining eligibility for the disability tax credit, the nature of the impairment,
with the exception of blindness, is irrelevant. What is significant for the purposes of
eligibility is the impact of the severe and prolonged impairment upon the ability to
carry out one or more 'basic activities of daily living.' These activities are defined in
the *Income Tax Act* as:

[3] The supporting person can only claim the disability tax credit as a transfer if the person with the disability is dependent on the supporting person
for the basic necessities of life (such as food, shelter or clothing).

- perceiving, thinking and remembering;
- feeding or dressing oneself;
- speaking so as to be understood, in a quiet setting, by another person familiar with the individual;
- hearing so as to understand, in a quiet setting, another person familiar with the individual;
- eliminating (bladder or bowel functions); and
- walking.

Individuals with a severe and prolonged impairment need not be markedly restricted in a basic activity of daily living to be eligible for the disability tax credit, provided that they would be markedly restricted if they were not receiving therapy that:

- is essential to sustain a vital function;
- is required to be administered at least three times each week for a total duration averaging not less than 14 hours a week; and
- cannot reasonably be expected to be of significant benefit to persons who are not so impaired.

The 2003 version of form T2201, *Disability Tax Credit Certificate*, is attached as Appendix 6. All persons wishing to establish eligibility for the credit must have the form completed and certified by an appropriate qualified practitioner.

Disability Tax Credit Claims

General

The number of disability tax credit self-claimants (i.e., those who claimed the disability tax credit for themselves) grew steadily from 1988 to 1994 (see Figure 2.1). This growth reflects the increased take-up of the credit following the expansion of eligibility in 1986. Prior to that time, the disability deduction (which predated the disability tax credit)[4] was available only to those who were blind or confined to a bed or who used a wheelchair.

After 1994, the number of disability tax credit self-claims remained fairly stable at approximately 380,000, until 2001, the latest year for which final data are available, when self-claims dropped to about 344,000. The decrease is attributable partly to the 2001 review of disability tax credit claims initiated by the Canada Revenue Agency (discussed later in this chapter).

Many tax filers who claim the disability tax credit for themselves do not need the full credit to reduce their federal tax to zero. Some of these individuals transfer all or some

---

[4] The 1988 tax reform converted a number of tax deductions, including the disability deduction, into credits.

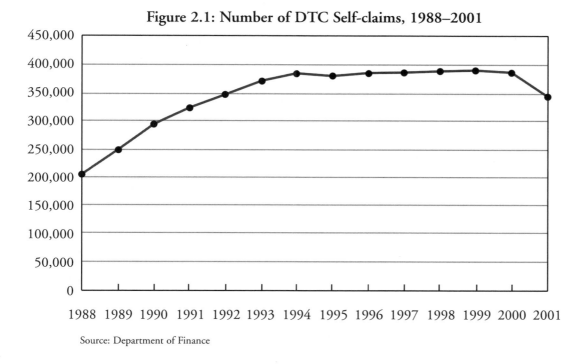

Figure 2.1: Number of DTC Self-claims, 1988–2001

Source: Department of Finance

portion of the credit to one or more supporting relatives. In 2001, about 75,000 Canadians claimed all or part of the disability tax credit as a transfer from a spouse, while 99,000 other supporting relatives claimed a transferred disability tax credit amount.

The total number of self-claims and transfers, however, does not reveal how many individuals are eligible for and claim the disability tax credit (or for whom a claim is made). The lack of clear data is due to the fact that two individuals, such as the person with a disability and the spouse, may each claim a portion of the credit.

The Department of Finance recently estimated that, in 2001, there were 400,000 Canadians eligible for the disability tax credit for whom a claim was made – either by the individuals themselves or a supporting spouse or relative, or both.[5]

The disability tax credit provided $330 million in federal tax relief to eligible individuals or their supporting relatives in 2001. This expenditure is a significant increase from previous years (see Figure 2.2),[6] despite the drop in the number of self-claims. The growth is due entirely to the increase in the credit amount from $4,293 to $6,000 in 2001. The Department of Finance projects that the amount of tax relief provided under the disability tax credit will rise to $375 million in 2004.

Disability Tax Fairness

[5] The Department of Finance recently conducted an evaluation of the disability tax credit, the results of which were published in the 2004 *Tax Expenditures and Evaluations* report.

[6] Figure 2.2 presents tax expenditure data in current dollars (i.e., not adjusted for inflation). When inflation is taken into account, the *real* tax expenditure declines modestly from 1993 to 1999.

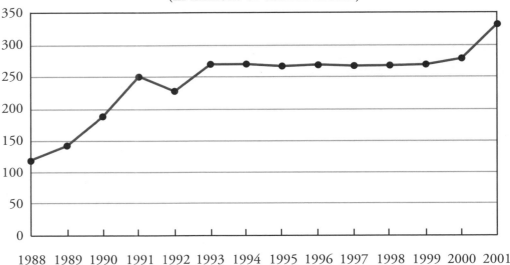

Figure 2.2: DTC Tax Expenditure, 1988–2001
(in millions of current dollars)

Source: Department of Finance

Age

One of the notable features about self-claimants of the disability tax credit is their age: more than half are seniors (see Table 2.1).[7] This has been the case since 1995 and the proportion of disability tax credit self-claimants who are age 65 or older has increased steadily in recent years (see Figure 2.3). Given that disability rates rise with age and that the proportion of seniors in the general population is growing, these figures are not surprising.[8]

Table 2.1: DTC Self-claims by Age, 2001

Age of tax filer	Number of DTC self-claims	% of DTC self-claims
< 25	4,900	1.4
25-34	12,800	3.7
35-44	24,500	7.1
45-54	39,200	11.4
55-64	54,900	16.0
65-74	70,400	20.5
75-84	86,500	25.2
85+	50,600	14.7
Total	**343,800**	**100.0**

Source: Department of Finance

[7] While only 1.5 percent of disability tax credit claimants are under age 25, most of the individuals eligible for the disability tax credit in this age group are likely children who would be claimed by their parents.

[8] It should be noted, however, that only a small fraction of seniors are eligible for the disability tax credit. Only 5 percent of tax filers age 65 or more claimed the disability tax credit in 2001. That said, some seniors who would be eligible for the disability tax credit may not claim it because they do not have to pay income tax.

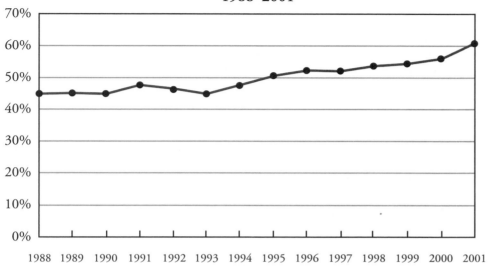

Figure 2.3: Percentage of DTC Self-Claimants Who Are Seniors, 1988–2001

Source: Department of Finance

A research paper[9] prepared for the Committee estimated that, as a result of the aging population, fully two-thirds of the disability tax credit recipients will be over 65 by 2031, with a near doubling of the total number of claimants by that date. This trend would lead to a doubling of the revenue cost of the disability tax credit in real terms (i.e., taking into account the effects of inflation). The result is that the disability tax credit increasingly will become a measure that provides tax relief to seniors, rather than to children and working age persons with disabilities. We explore this aspect of the disability tax credit in the Future Directions chapter.

Income

Persons with disabilities have lower incomes on average, generally as a result of lower rates of employment. This problem is reflected in the income distribution of disability tax credit self-claimants (see Table 2.2). Three-quarters of disability tax credit self-claimants had a total income for tax purposes of less than $30,000 in 2001, while only 5 percent had income above $60,000.

Disability Tax Fairness

[9] Smart and Stabile, *Tax Support for the Disabled in Canada*, 2003.

Table 2.2: DTC Self-claims by Total Income, 2001

Income of tax filer	Number of DTC self-claims	% of DTC self-claims
<$10,000	59,300	17.2
$10,000–$20,000	135,900	39.5
$20,000–$30,000	68,900	20.0
$30,000–$40,000	34,300	10.0
$40,000–$60,000	28,400	8.3
$60,000–$80,000	9,600	2.8
$80,000–$100,000	2,600	0.8
$100,000+	4,800	1.4
Total	**343,800**	**100.0**

Note: Total income refers to total income declared for tax purposes.
Source: Department of Finance

While this distribution is influenced by the high proportion of senior claimants, it is also worth noting that the average income of tax filers under age 65 who receive the disability tax credit is significantly lower than those not receiving it (see Table 2.3). For Canadians over age 65, the average recipient of the disability tax credit has about the same income as persons without disabilities.

In the case of seniors, one explanation for the fact that recipients of the disability tax credit have levels of income similar to those without disabilities is that a minimum income is provided to all seniors, regardless of disability, through Old Age Security and the Guaranteed Income Supplement. Another explanation is that because many seniors with a disability become functionally impaired only later in life, they are likely to have the same retirement incomes as those who do not become disabled (i.e., they had the same opportunities to work and save for retirement).

Table 2.3: Average Total Income by DTC Status and Age, 2001

Age	Average total income for DTC self-claimants	Average total income for others
Under 65	$20,881	$32,719
65 or older	$27,062	$27,517

Note: Total income refers to total income declared for tax purposes.
Source: Department of Finance

Concerns

The description of the disability tax credit sheds some light upon why this measure has been so difficult in its application. As noted, there are three components to the eligibility criteria: the presence of severe and prolonged impairment, its impact (a marked restriction) upon a basic activity of daily living and professional certification of the claim on a correctly completed form.

Various disability groups have expressed concerns for years about problems in the interpretation and application of the disability tax credit. But these issues came to the fore forcibly in 2001 when the Canada Revenue Agency[10] decided to conduct a mass audit of this credit (see box on next page).

The disability community was outraged by the way the 2001 review had been communicated and its extensive scope. It was also concerned about major revisions made throughout the 1990s to the T2201 form, which it felt made the interpretation of the eligibility criteria increasingly restrictive in many areas.

While a number of submissions to the Committee referred to the 2001 Canada Revenue Agency review, they also identified a broader range of issues related to the disability tax credit. These concerns can be grouped into two categories.

The first set involves the legislative policy and the interpretive issues associated with eligibility for the disability tax credit. The Department of Finance and the Canada Revenue Agency are responsible for the policy and legislation, and the interpretive aspects of the credit, respectively.

The second cluster of concerns relates to the administrative aspects of the disability tax credit, including the T2201, the process by which decisions are made and communicated to applicants, the procedures in place at various stages for reviewing these decisions, and the general lack of information provided to claimants regarding the appeals process and access to documents. The Canada Revenue Agency is responsible for the administration of the disability tax credit.

Our recommendations on the disability tax credit attempt to address the major eligibility and administrative issues identified. As discussed in the previous chapter, the social model of disability was a key influence on our deliberations and we consider our recommendations as a first step towards eligibility criteria that reflect the social model.

[10] Until December 2003, the Canada Revenue Agency was known as the Canada Customs and Revenue Agency.

Canada Revenue Agency Review of Disability Tax Credit Claims in 2001

Beginning in 1996, the Canada Revenue Agency adopted the administrative practice of reviewing all *Disability Tax Credit Certificates* (form T2201) for eligibility before assessing the tax return. This form of pre-qualification clearance is relatively unusual in the administration of the *Income Tax Act*. The Canada Revenue Agency has indicated that this practice has been adopted both to provide greater control over the granting of the credit and to avoid having to deny retroactively the claim to those who were granted it in error in previous years.

Because the Canada Revenue Agency lacked significant supporting information (and, in some cases, any information) on disability tax credit claimants who had first filed for the credit before 1996, the Agency decided in 2001 to seek better documentation of the claims from these 106,000 Canadian self-claimants. It did so by asking these individuals to re-qualify for the credit by having a qualified practitioner complete a new T2201 form. The Canada Revenue Agency excluded from this review those over age 75, spousal claims and those who claimed on behalf of other relatives.

The letter created apprehension and anger among members of the disability community. It stated: "After reviewing your file, we have determined that we do not have enough information to continue to allow your claim for the 2001 and future tax years."

The letter did not make clear that the Agency needed to obtain for its files additional data to support the claim. Nor did the letter intend to imply that the Agency had information that would disqualify the identified individual for the credit, although this intent might be read into its words. An estimated 17,000 individuals who received the letter did not file a new T2201 form, and approximately 31,500 claims that were filed were denied for those who previously had been considered eligible for the credit.

Our discussions on the disability tax credit went beyond what we are recommending. Most notably, we debated extensively incorporating the social model in the eligibility criteria for the disability tax credit. While we do not make any formal recommendation on the issue, we believe that our work in this area has broader application and warrants further examination. We discuss this in the Future Directions chapter.

Eligibility Concerns

a. Conceptualization of impairment

Submissions to the Committee raised several concerns related to the conceptualization of impairment. The current eligibility criteria, as set out in the *Income Tax Act* and the T2201 form, combine in one listing certain terms that pertain to human *functions* (e.g., speaking and hearing) and those that refer to *activities* (e.g., feeding or dressing). The result is that the present list of activities includes several human functions and, the Committee felt, a lack of clarity in the application of the criteria for the credit.

The terms hearing, speaking, eliminating, and perceiving, thinking and remembering all refer to *functions* necessary to carry out an activity. Activities, on the other hand, are purposeful and meaningful; they are intended to achieve a specific goal. A person must be able to learn, for example, in order to read and write. Feeding and dressing, by contrast, are *activities* that depend on several different physical and mental functions.

The failure to distinguish between functions and activities, and the resulting lack of clarity, have given rise, in our view, to confusion over the interpretation of a key eligibility criterion: a marked restriction in a basic activity of daily living. The Committee employed in our own deliberations a more rigorous conceptual distinction between human functions and basic activities of daily living, which we discuss further in Chapter 5.

As in the current disability tax credit, we agree that eligibility should require the presence of severe and prolonged impairment in *physical or mental functions*. This impairment, in turn, must give rise to *a marked restriction in activity*. While impairment in function is a necessary condition, its mere presence does not necessarily create a restriction in activity.

RECOMMENDATION 2.1

The Committee recommends that:

> The *Income Tax Act* be amended to replace the present wording 'severe and prolonged mental or physical impairment' with the wording 'severe and prolonged impairment in physical or mental functions.'

This recommendation is for clarification purposes and does not involve any revenue cost. It is not intended to alter the scope of eligibility for the credit.

---

b. Mental functions

Currently, eligibility for the disability tax credit of persons with an impairment in mental functions is recognized in the *Income Tax Act* through the term 'perceiving, thinking and remembering,' which is listed as basic activities of daily living. However, the Committee believes that the provisions of the Act were drafted at a time when the emphasis in respect of disabilities focused primarily upon physical disabilities, and impairments in mental functions were not as well recognized or understood.

Submissions to the Committee pointed out that persons with impairments in mental functions are at a disadvantage in eligibility determination because the symptoms and their associated impact have not been as well understood as impairments in physical functions. We were told that persons with intellectual impairments, learning disabilities and mood disorders generally have found it difficult in the past to qualify for the disability tax credit, even when their impairments have markedly restricted their activities of daily living.

In its submission to us, for example, the Coalition for Disability Tax Credit Reform quoted from testimony at the hearings held by the Sub-Committee on the Status of Persons with Disabilities: "From our experience, 100 percent of the new applications for [the disability tax credit] with people with schizophrenia have been rejected. Similar inconsistencies have been noted with respect to individuals with intellectual impairments."[11]

In addition, the Ontario Brain Injury Association noted that, in the absence of qualifying adverbs, the use of the term 'perceiving, thinking and remembering' created problems in application. Almost every human can perceive, think or remember to some degree. The simple presence of these functions provides no suitable threshold for eligibility determination.

"The question 'Can your patient perceive, think and remember?' is not a conclusive test to determine eligibility for individuals with mental impairments. Many psychiatrists, who are not familiar with case law, have refused to complete the T2201 [form] for their patients because they believe that the only correct response is 'yes,' regardless of the severity of the illness." – Coalition for Disability Tax Credit Reform

---

[11] Les Wall, President of the Schizophrenia Society, November 27, 2001.

34

Another problem is that the phrase 'perceiving, thinking and remembering' does not capture the full range of mental functions. For example, it conspicuously omits serious mood disorders. While some persons with a marked restriction in activity arising from a mental impairment qualify for the disability tax credit, others do not. Similar inconsistencies have been noted with respect to individuals with intellectual impairments.

Concerns regarding the eligibility of persons with learning disabilities were also brought to our attention. This form of disability is generally not well understood. It is entirely possible for a person to be of average or high intelligence and still have a severe learning disability that markedly restricts a basic activity of daily living.

In our view, learning is a critical dimension of thinking. In fact, the ability to learn involves several mental functions – namely, the ability to concentrate, perceive, remember and solve problems. The Committee believes that individuals with mood disorders and learning disabilities should be eligible for the disability tax credit in the same way as individuals with other impairments in mental functions.

Many of the eligibility concerns raised by the disability community and the House of Commons Standing Committee on Human Resources Development and the Status of Persons with Disabilities were not necessarily tied to the legislative wording of the eligibility criteria, but rather to how those criteria were interpreted and presented on form T2201 (see Appendix 6). The Canada Revenue Agency substantially revised the T2201 form for the 2003 tax year based on extensive consultations and focus-testing held during the summer of 2003 (see box on next page).

The revised form represents a substantial improvement over its predecessors – it indicates a better understanding of mental disability and should address many of the concerns raised with respect to the disability tax credit. There is room, however, for continued improvement in the form and for further consultation by the Canada Revenue Agency with the disability community.

The Committee believes that the term 'mental functions necessary for everyday life,' which is now being used on the T2201 form, is a clearer description of the effects of mental impairments. We propose that this terminology replace the term 'perceiving, thinking and remembering' in the current legislation.

2003 Revisions to the T2201 Form

In 2003, the Canada Revenue Agency held a major consultation over the course of five months with 22 organizations representing the disability community and health professionals that covered all aspects of the T2201 form.[12] The discussion proceeded on the basis that any change to the form required consensus and had to be consistent with the legislation. The resulting draft form was then focus-tested with qualified practitioners to determine whether the new form would be clear and easy to use.

The primary concern with the old form was that it simply asked the qualified practitioner completing the form a series of 'yes-no' questions with little scope to provide further supporting information regarding the effects of the individual's condition. As a result, this practice required the Agency to seek further clarification from a qualified practitioner when, if more detail had been provided on the form, further clarification would have been unnecessary. (In 2001, more than 40,000 clarification letters were sent to qualified practitioners.) Persons with impairments in mental functions were primarily affected. There were also concerns about whether the wording on the form was consistent with the criteria set out in the legislation.

As a result of the consultations, the T2201 form has been expanded to provide more information about the eligibility criteria. For most of the basic activities of daily living, the form first provides the legislative criteria, followed by information on how the criteria are interpreted and illustrative examples of what constitutes a marked restriction in that basic activity of daily living. Qualified practitioners are also invited to describe the effects of the impairment on the ability to perform a basic activity of daily living.

The most significant change in the T2201 form was the description of a marked restriction in perceiving, thinking and remembering. The form describes a marked restriction as being unable, or requiring an inordinate amount of time, to perform the mental functions necessary for everyday life, even with appropriate therapy, medication and devices. It then defines these mental functions as including memory, problem solving, goal setting and judgment, and adaptive functioning (e.g., abilities related to self-care, health and safety, social skills and common, simple transactions), and includes examples of each mental function.

---

[12] The Committee followed the consultation process and two Committee members were also participants in this process as representatives of disability organizations.

RECOMMENDATION 2.2

The Committee recommends that:

The term 'perceiving, thinking and remembering' as a basic activity of daily living in the *Income Tax Act* and on the T2201 form be replaced with the term 'mental functions necessary for everyday life.'

In our view, mental functions are the range of processes that govern how people think, feel and behave. Based on our consultations and research, they include memory, problem solving, judgment, perception, learning, attention, concentration, verbal and non-verbal comprehension and expression, and the regulation of behaviour and emotions. These functions are necessary for activities of everyday life that are required for self-care, health and safety, social skills and simple transactions.

This recommendation is for clarification purposes and does not involve any revenue cost. It is not intended to alter the scope of eligibility for the credit.

c. All or substantially all of the time

As noted, the eligibility requirement that a marked restriction must be present 'all or substantially all of the time' generally has been interpreted by the Canada Revenue Agency to mean that the symptoms that restrict activity are present 90 percent of the time or more.

The House of Commons Standing Committee on Human Resources Development and the Status of Persons with Disabilities had difficulty with this interpretation, arguing that it is too restrictive. In its December 2002 report, the Standing Committee noted that: "An individual who, for example, is unable to perform a basic activity of daily living 75 percent of the time is markedly restricted in this aspect of daily living."[13]

Our Committee discussed the use of the term 'all or substantially all' and its interpretation by the Canada Revenue Agency as the presence of symptoms that restrict activity 90 percent of the time or more. While we recognize that this 90 percent interpretation may work well for other tax measures that use the phrase 'all or substantially all,' there is a question as to whether this interpretation lends itself well to the disability tax credit, where eligibility needs to be determined in light of individual circumstances.

We considered the possible use of the term 'significant' instead of 'all or substantially all,' as it is less restrictive and more meaningful for health practitioners who complete the T2201 form. The term 'significant' would expand eligibility for the disability tax credit.

Disability Tax Fairness

[13] House of Commons Standing Committee on Human Resources Development and the Status of Persons with Disabilities, *Tax Fairness for Persons with Disabilities*, 2002, p. 16.

Even though use of the term 'significant' may be more meaningful for some, we could not reach consensus as to whether such a change would make the disability tax credit more fair. We discuss this issue further in Chapter 5.

Submissions to the Committee also pointed out that the current '90 percent rule' has created problems related to conditions with episodic manifestations. If the rule is interpreted to mean that symptoms of severe impairment must be present all or substantially all of the time, then individuals with conditions with intermittent symptoms could be disqualified from eligibility for the credit.

The Multiple Sclerosis Society pointed out in its submission to the Committee, for example, how its members may be affected by this interpretation. Multiple sclerosis is a disabling disease of the central nervous system. It often causes severe disablement – frequently intermittent – in the form of tremors, problems with balance, severe fatigue, cognitive impairment and paralysis.

Once diagnosed, individuals must cope with the disease for the rest of their lives. But the condition is unpredictable in terms of how it affects daily living and how it progresses over time. Periods of spontaneous recovery may be interrupted by erratic disabling attacks. The result can be a permanent restriction in activities even though the symptoms are not always present; individuals cannot undertake some activity where a sudden onset of symptoms could pose a danger to themselves or others.

Similarly, the Canadian AIDS Society noted in its submission that persons with HIV experience recurring and unpredictable periods of good health and poor health despite having an illness that is permanent.

Many disabilities related to mental function, such as schizophrenia, brain injury and learning disabilities, can represent severe and prolonged impairments in mental functions – as the eligibility criteria for the disability tax credit require. However, many applications involving these impairments have been rejected for eligibility. While the condition is continuous, some of the disabling symptoms may not be present all of the time.

Persons with bipolar disorder, for example, may not be continually depressed or psychotic. Alternatively, or in addition, their depression or disordered thinking might vary in intensity. Even when less or not depressed, their judgment and problem-solving ability may be impaired and restrict their functioning. The unpredictable expression and resurgence of symptoms requires careful life management, which typically means that these individuals can be markedly restricted in their ability to carry out a basic activity all or substantially all of the time.

In our view, *a marked restriction* means that even with therapy, medication and/or devices, relative to someone of similar chronological age and for a substantial amount of time, an individual cannot independently perform one or more basic activities of daily living or requires an inordinate amount of time to carry out independently such activities.

A severe and prolonged impairment with continuously expressed symptoms (e.g., blindness or paraplegia) can lead to a marked restriction in activity (e.g., sight, walking) and a severe and prolonged impairment with intermittent symptoms of varying intensity (e.g., schizophrenia or dementia) can lead to a marked restriction in activity (e.g., mental functions). The Committee believes that individuals with both types of symptoms can be eligible for the disability tax credit under a proper interpretation of the present legislation and that this view is consistent with the wording on the current form, although this interpretation should be clarified further.

RECOMMENDATION 2.3

The Committee recommends that:

The Canada Revenue Agency state in its explanatory materials and on the application form for the disability tax credit that some impairments in function can result in a marked restriction in a basic activity of daily living, even though these impairments may have signs and symptoms that may be intermittent.

This action is not intended to alter the legislative requirement that a marked restriction in a basic activity of daily living be present 'all or substantially all of the time.' This recommendation should not involve any revenue cost.

d. Marked restriction

For the purposes of the disability tax credit, the assessment of a marked restriction requires qualified practitioners to make judgments about the effects of severe and prolonged impairment in function upon the ability to carry out a basic activity of daily living. In making this assessment, they should take into consideration the relevant context.

Two people with the same diagnosis or impairment may not be restricted in activity in precisely the same way. Their restrictions result from their impairment within the context of individual factors and societal factors, such as access to disability supports or the extent of accommodation.

e. Cumulative effects

In some cases, one or more severe and prolonged impairments may result in the significant restriction of more than one basic activity of daily living without the individual being markedly restricted in any one of such basic activities all or substantially all of the time. The House of Commons Standing Committee on Human Resources Development and the Status of Persons with Disabilities also suggested that it might be appropriate for a person who is restricted in more than one basic activity of daily living, but not all or substantially all of the time in any one of these activities, to be considered eligible for the disability tax credit because of the cumulative impact of such restrictions.[14]

"The current wording of the Income Tax Act discriminates against those who have a combination of disabling conditions that act together to create a marked restriction when viewed holistically." – BC Coalition of People with Disabilities

There are many circumstances in which individuals are restricted in carrying out two or more basic activities of daily living. However, in cases where these individuals are not markedly restricted in carrying out any single activity, they are not currently eligible

---

[14] House of Commons Standing Committee on Human Resources Development and the Status of Persons with Disabilities, *Tax Fairness for Persons with Disabilities*, 2002, pp. 16–17.

for the disability tax credit. This is true even if the cumulative effects of the individuals' restrictions are equivalent to the effects of having a marked restriction in a single activity all or substantially all of the time.

The Committee felt strongly that fairness requires that taxpayers who face these cumulative restrictions in their ability to carry out basic activities of daily living that are equivalent to the effects of having a marked restriction in a single activity all or substantially all of the time should also qualify for the disability tax credit. For example, individuals with multiple sclerosis who experience fatigue, depressed mood and balance problems may not be *markedly* restricted in a single activity of daily living such as walking. However, the combination of symptoms may create a marked restriction because several activities like walking, dressing and mental functions are affected, even if each single activity is not markedly restricted.

RECOMMENDATION 2.4

The Committee recommends that:

The *Income Tax Act* be amended to provide that persons with a severe and prolonged impairment who are restricted in two or more basic activities of daily living qualify for the disability tax credit if the cumulative effects of the restriction are equivalent to a marked restriction in a single basic activity of daily living all or substantially all of the time.

This recommendation is estimated to involve a revenue cost of approximately $50 million annually.

It is important to note that this recommendation does not alter the requirement that the impairment be severe and prolonged. Persons with multiple impairments, none of which is severe and prolonged or the effects of which are not present all or substantially all of the time, will not qualify for the disability tax credit.

The Committee feels that this recommendation is consistent with the unanimous vote in the House of Commons on November 20, 2002, which called upon the government to level the playing field for Canadians with disabilities and incorporate in a more humane and compassionate manner the real-life circumstances of persons with disabilities in eligibility criteria for the disability tax credit.

f. Life-sustaining therapy
As noted, individuals who would be markedly restricted in a basic activity of daily living if they did not receive life-sustaining therapy are eligible for the disability tax credit.

This provision dates from the 2000 federal budget. The purpose of this provision was to extend the disability tax credit only to situations in which the amount of time dedicated to the therapy significantly restricted the individual's ability to undertake normal, everyday activities. The legislation requires that the therapy be administered at least three times per week and that individuals spend, on average, 14 hours per week – the equivalent of two hours each day – receiving life-sustaining therapy in order to qualify for the disability tax credit. However, the term 'therapy' is not defined in the *Income Tax Act* and there are questions as to what might be included in the time taken to receive such therapy.

There are individuals with severe conditions who require considerable time to receive therapy who may not be eligible for the disability tax credit, given the Canada Revenue Agency's interpretation of therapy. In particular, several submissions to the Committee raised the issue of the application of the life-sustaining therapy provisions to children with Type 1 diabetes mellitus (or insulin-dependent diabetes).

For Type 1 diabetics, life-sustaining therapy currently is considered to be insulin injection. A number of other ancillary activities, such as monitoring blood sugar levels, are not deemed by the Canada Revenue Agency to comprise the administration of the therapy and therefore are not counted toward the three-times-per-week and 14-hour-per-week requirements.

Insulin can be delivered either by means of multiple daily injections or by continuous infusion through an insulin pump. At the present time, individuals using a continuous infusion pump qualify for the disability tax credit if this mode of insulin administration is a medical necessity.

In addition, the Committee noted that there are recent decisions of the Tax Court of Canada in which judges have interpreted therapy to include some ancillary activities in determining that a child with Type 1 diabetes was eligible for the disability tax credit. These Court decisions have recognized that some children with Type 1 diabetes, because of the time devoted to their therapy, are not able to participate in everyday activities to the same extent and in the same manner as others who do not require life-sustaining therapy.

The Committee believes that the principles in these Court decisions should guide the government in developing any required policy and administrative changes regarding life-sustaining therapy. The Canada Revenue Agency could issue an interpretation bulletin, for example, indicating that life-sustaining therapy includes activities, such as monitoring of blood sugar levels and determining insulin dosages, as indicated in recent Tax Court decisions.

The concerns of parents caring for a child with Type 1 diabetes raise a broader issue: Is the disability tax credit the right vehicle to address the challenges these families face? We discuss the limitations of the tax system further in Chapter 5, Future Directions.

RECOMMENDATION 2.5

The Committee recommends that:

The federal government ensure that the legislative and administrative requirements concerning the present interpretation regarding life-sustaining therapy adequately reflect the time taken for essential preparation, administration of and necessary recovery from life-sustaining therapy as recently interpreted in decisions of the Tax Court of Canada.

The revenue cost of this recommendation will ultimately depend on the nature of the changes implemented by the government.

---

g. Qualified practitioners

The *Income Tax Act* and the T2201 form set out a list of qualified practitioners who currently may certify the presence of a marked restriction in a basic activity of daily living or the receipt of life-sustaining therapy. The list includes medical doctors (all activities), optometrists (vision), audiologists (hearing), occupational therapists (walking, feeding and dressing), psychologists (perceiving, thinking and remembering) and speech language pathologists (speaking).[15]

The Canadian Physiotherapy Association, in its submission to the Committee, asked that physiotherapists be added to the list of qualified practitioners authorized to certify walking or mobility impairments. The Association explained that physiotherapy is a primary care, self-regulated health profession committed to client-centred services. It also stated that the addition of physiotherapists to the list of qualified practitioners who can certify walking or mobility impairments would provide Canadians with an alternate accessible and reliable resource for certification of their eligibility for the disability tax credit.

"Including physiotherapists in the list of [qualified practitioners] would significantly reduce the difficulties individuals with disabilities face by allowing the health professional who often has the most in-depth knowledge of their impairment history and prognosis to verify their impairment." – Canadian Physiotherapy Association

---

[15] The Committee recommends replacing the phrase 'perceiving, thinking and remembering' with the phrase 'mental functions necessary for everyday life' (see Recommendation 2.2). Medical doctors and psychologists would continue to be allowed to certify this type of marked restriction.

Another key issue raised in submissions was access to qualified practitioners in remote and northern communities.

"The definition of [qualified practitioner] to fill out [form T2201] should be expanded to include nurse practitioners, as many remote communities in the NWT lack doctors and other medical professionals. Nurses are often the only medical people in the community."
– Northwest Territories Council of Persons with Disabilities

Nurse practitioners act as the primary delivery agents of health care in remote, rural and northern regions of the country. The Committee recognizes that the provision of health care throughout the country is evolving increasingly into various forms of collaborative practice in which nurse practitioners play a central role within a team of health professionals. However, the Committee was informed that there is no consistent definition of the role of nurse practitioners across the country and that more work would be required to determine under what circumstances nurse practitioners should be allowed to certify eligibility for the disability tax credit.

RECOMMENDATION 2.6

The Committee recommends that:

The *Income Tax Act* be amended to include physiotherapists in the list of qualified practitioners eligible to certify for the purposes of the disability tax credit a marked restriction in walking.

The federal government consult with the Canadian Nurses Association to determine under what circumstances nurse practitioners could be allowed to certify eligibility for the disability tax credit.

This recommendation does not involve any revenue cost.

Administrative Concerns

Submissions to the Committee raised a wide range of concerns regarding the administration of the disability tax credit. Many of these concerns relate to the fact that the disability tax credit is more complex to administer than a number of other personal income tax provisions.

Taxpayers qualify for the age credit, for example, when they turn 65. Eligibility for the Canada Child Tax Benefit is determined by two clear factors: number of children up to and including age 18 and level of household net income. While the medical expense tax credit has its own complexities, it basically allows only certain defined medically necessary or disability-related items to be claimed, all of which must be backed up by a receipt.

However, the eligibility criteria for the disability tax credit involve a determination about a relatively subjective state – a marked restriction in a basic activity of daily living.

When the Canada Revenue Agency receives a T2201 form, Agency staff first verify that the form has been completely filled out as required. If not, it is sent back to the individual for completion.

If the form is complete, staff of the Canada Revenue Agency then review the form to see if it clearly indicates whether or not the individual meets the disability tax credit eligibility criteria. This determination may involve referral to medical advisory staff at Agency headquarters. If the form does not make a clear case for eligibility, the Canada Revenue Agency will seek clarification from the qualified practitioner who filled out the form. Once the Agency has clear information, it makes a determination as to whether the individual is eligible for the disability tax credit on either a temporary or indeterminate basis.

Applicants denied the disability tax credit who are dissatisfied with the decision or have additional information regarding their application may contact the Canada Revenue Agency and ask to have a second review carried out of the decision in their case. Under this process, a different staff member reviews the claim and either confirms or reverses the initial determination. While this second review process would appear to be available on request, unfortunately taxpayers are not automatically told of its existence, and hence may not have the opportunity to take advantage of this further step in the review process. To ensure fairness, the Canada Revenue Agency must ensure that taxpayers are fully informed of the availability of a second review of their disability tax credit claim.

If the claim is denied, the claimant may choose to file a Notice of Objection, which is the formal means of informing the Canada Revenue Agency that the claimant disagrees with its decision. The Appeals Branch of the Canada Revenue Agency then reviews the claim and either reassesses in favour of the individual or confirms the earlier denial. Claimants who wish to pursue the matter further in the event that the claim is still denied may appeal the decision to the Tax Court of Canada. Both the claimant and the Canada Revenue Agency can appeal an unfavourable decision of the Tax Court to the Federal Court of Appeal.

a. General concerns

This section presents only the highlights of the concerns brought to our attention regarding this administrative process. These relate to the T2201 form itself, the clarification letters sent to qualified practitioners, the failure to give detailed reasons for rejection of an application and the process for resolving objections by persons with disabilities to the Canada Revenue Agency's determination of their eligibility for the disability tax credit.

The Committee learned, for example, that there were inconsistencies in the way that disability tax credit claims were adjudicated. We were told that Canada Revenue Agency staff may have made judgments about medical issues without obtaining additional or any medical evidence. Further, some persons who had a qualified practitioner certify their marked restriction have been denied the disability tax credit without being provided any details about the refusal other than a standard and very general explanation.

This problem was pointed out to us by the Coalition for Disability Tax Credit Reform, which expressed concern in its submission about the lack of specific reasons for refusing a disability tax credit claim. Without these details, applicants are at a serious disadvantage if they wish to file a Notice of Objection.

The Committee notes that the Canada Revenue Agency is currently reviewing the content of the letters it sends to individuals whose claims have been denied, using the same consultative process with the disability community that was used for the revisions to the T2201 form.

In addition, many applicants and qualified practitioners believe that a physician or other health professional at the Canada Revenue Agency adjudicates the claims or reviews the additional information provided by the qualified practitioner. Indeed, this generally is not the case. With this background, a significant number of applicants may choose not to object to the decision. They are not likely to file a Notice of Objection indicating their intent to question the decision.

Concerns about the reliability of the assessment are reinforced by the rate of reversal in decisions arising from a Notice of Objection filing. From 1996–97 to 2002–03 fiscal years, close to 50 percent of the 15,000 Notices of Objection relating to the disability tax credit filed with the Appeals Branch of the Canada Revenue Agency were reassessed in favour of the taxpayer. When reassessing a claim, the Appeals Branch may take into account new information provided by the taxpayer, such as an updated T2201 form.

Many of these issues relate to the period prior to the 2003 consultations and the efforts made by the Canada Revenue Agency to improve its administrative practices.

Indeed, the Agency recently has improved its processes relating to the disability tax credit, in several cases by following more carefully its own stated procedures and guidelines, which are outlined in Taxation Operations Manuals.

Concerns have been raised as to whether Canada Revenue Agency staff have always followed the guidelines on disability-related tax measures outlined in these manuals. Further questions have been asked about whether persons with disabilities can obtain accurate information about disability-related tax measures from general Canada Revenue Agency staff.

The challenge for the Canada Revenue Agency is to ensure more consistent and appropriate implementation of its procedures. Improved training of staff and adherence to policies and procedures when adjudicating claims should address many of the identified problems. Ideally, these practices will also reduce the number of appeals of eligibility decisions.

RECOMMENDATION 2.7

The Committee recommends that:

The Canada Revenue Agency:
- **ensure that its staff follow the procedures relating to the disability tax credit in its Taxation Operations Manuals and Interpretation Bulletins;**
- **ensure that its general staff are able to assist persons with disabilities with respect to completing and filing the T2201 form, or refer them to appropriate specialized personnel where required;**
- **develop training programs, workshops and guidelines for its staff regarding changes to the legislation and interpretive guidelines for the disability tax credit, and the administration of tax measures for persons with disabilities;**
- **develop appropriate communications and educational material for qualified practitioners to assist them in completing the T2201 form;**
- **make clear in its communication materials that a second informal review is available to taxpayers denied the disability tax credit; and**
- **monitor the achievement of these recommendations.**

Elements of this recommendation that are consistent with current practice do not involve any revenue cost. The Committee estimates that about $2 million annually will be required to implement the components of this recommendation that represent new initiatives.

b. T2201 form

As noted, the *Income Tax Act* and Canada Revenue Agency guidelines require applicants for the disability tax credit to complete a form known as the *Disability Tax Credit Certificate*, commonly referred to as the T2201 form. Over the past decade, the T2201 form has been modified several times – resulting in a generally more stringent interpretation of the 'marked restriction' criterion. However, the latest version of the T2201, issued for the 2003 tax year, is clearer and easier to follow and reflects more closely, in our view, the intent of the *Income Tax Act*.

The Committee supports the process used to arrive at the current form. We want to ensure the continuation of the progress achieved through this widespread consultation and review. In order to track the impact of the changes, the Committee proposes that the Canada Revenue Agency carry out focus-testing beyond those groups involved in the initial discussions to determine whether the revised form reflects its broader intent and is easier to use. The focus tests should determine the satisfaction level with the new form among qualified practitioners and taxpayers who have used it in the current year.

In addition to this feedback, the Canada Revenue Agency should institute better procedures for providing annual detailed statistics on the number of claims and their disposition, including data on the status of accepted claims over a lengthy time period. This tracking should involve the preparation of a profile of eligible disability tax credit claimants and the impact of the revised form. Further, it would be useful to have some data on claims processing broken down by relevant basic activity of daily living.

This information should be available as part of the ongoing consultation process so that the disability community can better understand and review the actual administration of the credit.

RECOMMENDATION 2.8

The Committee recommends that:

The Canada Revenue Agency continue to improve the T2201 form by ensuring that:

- **its ongoing consultations involve a wide representation of consumers and qualified practitioners regarding the T2201 form or related disability tax credit materials such as clarification letters and letters to individuals whose claim has been denied;**
- **the guidelines relating to the completion of the form are clear and concise to enable claimants and qualified practitioners to understand the eligibility criteria for the disability tax credit;**
- **examples and questions on the T2201 form reflect real-life situations to enable an appropriate determination of the severity of the impairment;**
- **examples and questions on the T2201 form continue to be revised as necessary and appropriate to reflect changes in legislation and court decisions; and**
- **data are collected, in order to evaluate the impact of the revisions to the T2201 form, on the number and percentage of successful and unsuccessful claims by basic activity of daily living, and claims for which additional information was requested (clarification letters) by basic activity of daily living.**

This recommendation is largely consistent with current practice and would involve only minor costs.

c. Clarification letters

Several problems were also brought to our attention regarding clarification letters sent by the Canada Revenue Agency to qualified practitioners requesting additional information about their clients. Many questions in the clarification letters are too general and are not always relevant to the specific disability of the individual.

The Canada Revenue Agency has a practice of sending to the claimant a copy of the clarification letter it is sending to the qualified practitioner. The purpose of this practice is to provide the claimant the opportunity to discuss the issues with the qualified practitioner. The Committee encourages the Agency to continue this practice.

RECOMMENDATION 2.9

The Committee recommends that:

The Canada Revenue Agency take the following steps with respect to clarification letters:

- **specify in writing why clarification is required in order to help qualified practitioners address specific issues or concerns; and**
- **ensure that all questions are relevant to the specific disability, instead of using a uniform approach for all impairments.**

This recommendation does not involve any additional cost.

d. Dispute resolution

Not surprisingly, many applicants are confused when their claim is rejected. Most expect a positive result when a qualified practitioner has certified their claim (and perhaps even received payment to complete the T2201 form and the clarification letters).

Many individuals with disabilities are often too intimidated or discouraged to challenge the refusal of their claim for a disability tax credit. Persons with a serious impairment in mental functions, in particular, do not always have the capacity or stamina to file an objection.

On paper, exemplary procedures are in place to ensure transparency, fairness and respectful treatment of applicants whose claim has been denied. While these procedures are set out in the Canada Revenue Agency publication *Appeals Renewal Initiative* and the pamphlet *Resolving Your Dispute – A more open, transparent process*, many persons with disabilities may not understand their rights and the recourse process (objection and appeal) open to them. These individuals may not know they have the right to access documents in their file, as identified in the pamphlet.

The Canada Revenue Agency already has good principles and processes in place to deal with taxpayers who wish to dispute its decisions. But the principles sometimes fail to be put into practice.

RECOMMENDATION 2.10

The Committee recommends that:

The Canada Revenue Agency intensify its existing efforts to ensure that:
- **taxpayers who receive a letter denying their disability tax credit claims be:**
  - **(i) given specific reasons for the denial,**
  - **(ii) informed about their objection and appeal rights through a copy of the pamphlet, *Your Appeal Rights Under the Income Tax Act*, provided by the Agency,**
  - **(iii) informed that other persons, such as family members, friends or professional advisors, can act on their behalf, and**
  - **(iv) informed that they have access to documents in their file when the Canada Revenue Agency acknowledges receipt of the Notice of Objection, through a copy of the pamphlet, *Resolving your dispute – A more open, transparent process*, provided by the Agency;**
- **appeals officers have access, if required, to competent medical advice when reviewing Notices of Objection and additional medical reports; and**
- **appeals officers meet with taxpayers or their representative in appropriate cases.**

This recommendation should involve only minor incremental costs.

As part of its efforts to create a general transparent redress mechanism, the Canada Revenue Agency launched an Appeals Renewal Initiative in December 1997. The purpose of the initiative was to inform Canadians about the Agency's internal dispute resolution service.

The Canada Revenue Agency has recently re-established an Appeals Advisory Committee and the Agency has informed us that it intends to have representation from the disability community on this committee. We strongly support the need for such a mechanism to monitor the effectiveness of the Canada Revenue Agency's internal review procedures.

Even after exhausting the objection process, taxpayers who are still dissatisfied with the decision regarding their case can appeal to the Tax Court of Canada. While the Tax Court will always be available as an option, ideally it should be used only as a last resort after other methods of dispute resolution have been tried.

Appealing a disability tax credit claim to Tax Court can be an intimidating and expensive process for many taxpayers. Yet the disability tax credit is worth a relatively modest amount of money compared with other programs for persons with disabilities – a maximum $1,038 in federal tax savings for 2004.

The majority of persons with disabilities who might wish to appeal to the Tax Court cannot afford the costs involved in an appeal. Further, appealing a case to the Tax Court may not be a practical solution for persons with disabilities since it may not be readily accessible, for example, to many individuals who live in northern or rural communities, especially when the disability prohibits travel.

There may be alternative and informal dispute resolution processes that can be a practical means of resolving tax disputes without relying on costly and time-consuming litigation. The Committee explored the possibility of applying one specific alternative method, known as 'mediation,' to disputes related to the disability tax credit in particular.

Mediation is a collaborative approach, which typically involves lower cost and less stress than going to court. While we support the need for more cooperative processes for resolving disputes, the Committee agreed that mediation was likely not the best approach for the disability tax credit, which involves a 'yes' or 'no' decision rather than a negotiated compromise.

We propose, instead, the creation of some form of alternative dispute resolution process that would be available after a decision by the Appeals Branch to deny the disability tax credit claim and confirm a negative Notice of Assessment. This proposed alternative dispute resolution process would not require formal rules of evidence or procedure. It may not be necessary, for example, for a hearing to be held in every case: issues might be dealt with by correspondence or telephone.

RECOMMENDATION 2.11

The Committee recommends that:

The Canada Revenue Agency develop an alternative dispute resolution process for disability tax credit claims following an Appeals Branch denial, relying on an informal but independent process based on basic fairness criteria.

The Canada Revenue Agency mount a pilot project to test the operation of the suggested alternative dispute resolution process.

This pilot project is estimated to cost $4 million over one to two years. Ongoing costs would depend on the results of this pilot project.

The process we are suggesting would not – nor is it intended to – duplicate the procedures in place when appealing to the Tax Court. This process should be much more informal in terms of its structure, access, procedures and other features. The taxpayer would likely not incur significant costs with this alternative dispute resolution process.

Our suggestion is for an independent arbitrator who would hear from both the claimant and the Canada Revenue Agency and would then recommend whether the disability tax credit claim should be allowed or denied. Arbitrators should be legal or tax professionals, such as tax practitioners or law professors, who would be expected to apply the provisions of the *Income Tax Act* in making their decisions. The Canada Revenue Agency would appoint the arbitrators from a list, which could be drawn up by the Agency and the proposed advisory committee on disability and taxation (see Recommendation 2.12).

The recommendation of the arbitrator would not be binding on the Canada Revenue Agency or the taxpayer. The Canada Revenue Agency could still deny the disability tax credit and appeals to the Tax Court would continue to be available to the taxpayer. It is expected, however, that relatively few cases would be taken to the Tax Court after a decision arising from this process.

e. Advisory committee

Our Committee has made several recommendations to improve the administration of the disability tax credit. Our final recommendation in that respect is to form a consultative committee to oversee the implementation and monitoring of our previous recommendations.

RECOMMENDATION 2.12

The Committee recommends that:

In order to deal with the administrative aspects of the disability tax credit and the achievement of the previously enumerated recommendations, the Canada Revenue Agency form a consultative committee composed of consumer and professional representatives that would report directly to the Minister of National Revenue on all administrative aspects of the tax system related to persons with disabilities.

This recommendation should involve only minor costs.

Awareness of the Disability Tax Credit

A key question that the Committee addressed is whether Canadians who are potentially eligible for the disability tax credit actually receive it. Because the disability tax credit is available only to those with a severe and prolonged impairment that markedly restricts their ability to perform a basic activity of daily living, it is claimed by a relatively small proportion of persons who might be identified as having some form of disability.

In its evaluation of the disability tax credit, the Department of Finance determined that the disability tax credit appears to be reaching its target population. Using data from the Participation and Activity Limitation Survey and the National Population Health Survey, the Department calculated that the potential disability tax credit-recipient population was between 306,000 and 473,000.

As noted, the Department of Finance estimated using tax data that claims were made by or on behalf of approximately 400,000 individuals with severe and prolonged impairments in 2001. This estimate excludes some potential recipients of the disability tax credit who are better off foregoing the disability tax credit and including all of their attendant care or nursing home expenses in their medical expense tax credit claim (an estimated 22,000).[16] Adding these individuals leads to an estimate of potential disability tax credit recipients of 422,000. This number is well within the range estimated using data from the two surveys.

Despite these figures, data from the Participation and Activity Limitation Survey indicate that, in the 2000 tax year, a significant proportion of the individuals covered in the survey either were unaware of the credit or did not know whether they had claimed the credit.[17]

A related issue frequently raised in submissions to the Committee was the argument that individuals who receive disability benefits under the Canada Pension Plan (CPP) should

---

[16]Under the *Income Tax Act*, individuals eligible for the disability tax credit cannot claim the disability tax credit when they claim attendant care or nursing home expenses in excess of $10,000 under the medical expense tax credit.

[17]Statistics Canada, *Disability Supports in Canada, 2001 – Tables*, Catalogue no. 89-581-XIE, 2003, pp. 119, 130.

also be eligible for the disability tax credit.[18] Having gone through the process of qualifying for CPP disability benefits, many groups felt that these individuals should automatically receive the disability tax credit.

More specifically, these groups felt that it should not be necessary to fill out separate forms for the Canada Pension Plan as well as the disability tax credit. In fact, the Coalition for Disability Tax Credit Reform proposed a simplification of the application process for both programs as a preliminary step in their harmonization. Tax return data show that only a fraction of CPP disability beneficiaries receive the disability tax credit. In 2001, an estimated 24 percent of those individuals made a self-claim for the disability tax credit, meaning that about 220,000 of them did not claim the disability tax credit.[19]

Why is such a small proportion of Canada Pension Plan disability beneficiaries benefiting from the disability tax credit? One key reason is that the disability tax credit and CPP disability benefits have different purposes. The disability tax credit recognizes the effect of a severe and prolonged disability on an individual's ability to pay tax because of disability-related costs. Canada Pension Plan disability benefits provide income replacement for individuals who are unable to continue working as a result of a prolonged disability.

This difference in objectives leads to distinct eligibility criteria. Under the disability tax credit, applicants must be markedly restricted all or substantially all of the time in their ability to perform a basic activity of daily living, even with the use of aids, medication or therapy. By contrast, workers may be eligible for CPP disability benefits if they are incapable of regularly pursuing any substantially gainful occupation due to a severe and prolonged disability, and regardless of whether they have a severe and prolonged impairment resulting in a marked restriction in a basic activity of daily living.

As a result, some individuals who qualify for the disability tax credit may not be eligible for Canada Pension Plan disability benefits and vice versa. For example, persons who use a wheelchair may qualify for the disability tax credit, but would not be eligible for CPP disability benefits if they were able to work. (There is a large group of disability tax credit recipients who do not qualify for CPP disability benefits because they do not have sufficient history in the workforce, or because they are over age 65, which is when CPP disability benefits convert to CPP retirement benefits.)

Despite these explanations, the Committee still considered the proportion of Canada Pension Plan disability beneficiaries who make a disability tax credit claim to be unusually low, even taking into account the different eligibility criteria for the two measures. Because the two programs are administered separately, we could only speculate

[18] The province of Quebec operates its own similar plan, the Quebec Pension Plan.

[19] Based on data provided by the Department of Finance.

as to the reason why so many CPP disability beneficiaries do not receive the disability tax credit. It is possible that there is a knowledge gap as to potential eligibility for the disability tax credit.

With this in mind, the Committee believes that it is essential first to determine the reason for the problem, if any, and then to identify possible solutions for increasing the take-up rate amongst CPP disability beneficiaries of the disability tax credit. (The taxability of Canada Pension Plan disability benefits is discussed in Chapter 3.)

RECOMMENDATION 2.13

The Committee recommends that:

The Canada Revenue Agency, in conjunction with the appropriate departments, undertake a review of Canada Pension Plan disability beneficiaries and disability tax credit claimants with the goal of evaluating possible reasons for the low take-up of the disability tax credit by CPP disability beneficiaries.

The Canada Revenue Agency work with other government departments to ensure that all applicants for CPP disability benefits are advised of their potential eligibility for the disability tax credit, and furnished with forms and information so that they can readily consider their eligibility and make an application for the disability tax credit if appropriate. If, as a result of this work, the government finds that there is a significant overlap in eligibility, it should explore whether a simplified application process or joint administration of some aspects of the two programs is warranted.

This recommendation has an unknown revenue cost. Additional tax relief offered through the disability tax credit arising from this recommendation should already be provided under existing legislation. This recommendation should involve only minor administrative costs.

Other Possible Changes to the Disability Tax Credit

The Committee noted a number of other suggestions for longer-term changes in the disability tax credit. In one paper prepared for the Committee,[20] a modification was outlined to achieve greater equity between those disability tax credit claimants whose disability-related expenses were largely non-itemizable, and who therefore received only the disability tax credit, and those claimants whose disability expenses were largely itemized medical costs, who received both the disability tax credit and the medical expense tax credit.

---

[20] Smart and Stabile, *Tax Support for the Disabled in Canada*, 2003.

Under an example illustrating this suggestion, the existing disability tax credit amount would be split into a basic amount – say $4,000 – and a supplementary amount – say $2,500. All eligible qualified disability tax credit claimants would receive both amounts, but would be allowed to claim a medical expense tax credit only to the extent that their eligible medical expenses exceeded the supplementary credit amount of $2,500.

The change would mean that those with few or no itemizable costs would continue to receive the same amount of tax relief, while those with a heavy balance of itemizable costs would receive a modestly lower credit. However they would still, in most cases, have all of their relevant expenses recognized.

Beyond the Disability Tax Credit

The Committee believes that the current disability tax credit provides important support to persons with disabilities, and that such support can be justified on the basis of tax equity. However, the disability tax credit is at best a blunt instrument, delivering a largely uniform benefit to individuals with sharply varying degrees of impairment, needs and additional non-itemizable costs.

As a result, it is difficult to justify the disability tax credit as a means of ensuring that persons with disabilities can participate fully in society. Effective assistance to enable full participation is better provided through tailored programs of support, administered through expenditure programs on an individualized basis and not through an instrument that, by its very nature, is inappropriate as a social policy vehicle.

In a federation such as Canada, such national programs of direct assistance to individuals require cooperation among various levels of government. The disability tax credit by itself should therefore not be viewed as the answer to the needs and aspirations of persons with disabilities but rather as one component of a broad range of supports and equity. The substantial improvements to such programs that are required in future to enable full participation appear to rest, in large part, on individually tailored programs of support in expenditure programs rather than on broad tax measures that are invariably insensitive to diverse needs.

Furthermore, the Committee recognizes that more than half of the benefits from the existing disability tax credit flow to those over 65, and this proportion will increase as Canada's population ages. The requirements of seniors with disabilities deserve recognition, but the Committee believes that these are best addressed within measures designed specifically for the country's rapidly aging population.

Because the disability tax credit is an important element in recognizing the needs of persons with disabilities, the Committee is recommending measures to clarify the existing disability tax credit and to make it more fair and accessible. We believe that such changes are justified on the basis of both equity and the needs of persons with disabilities.

But while the disability tax credit is important and improvements in its scope and fairness are essential, the credit by itself cannot provide the type of recognition and supports required by persons with disabilities. We are therefore recommending no general increase in the amount of the disability tax credit (above any automatic increases in light of inflation).

Rather, we feel strongly that additional available resources should largely be channelled into programs that can deliver benefits more effectively. Ideally, the Committee would like to see the disability tax credit play relatively less of a role in the system of supports to persons with disabilities. In Chapter 5, we recommend that any new substantial funding to promote fairness and inclusion for persons with disabilities not be allocated to tax measures.

Chapter 3:
Employment- and Education- Related Tax Measures

Chapter 3: Employment- and Education-Related Tax Measures

Introduction

As noted in Chapter 1 on context, the Committee placed a high priority on promoting the inclusion of persons with disabilities through participation in education and employment. This objective is consistent with the federal government's statement, outlined in the February 2004 Speech from the Throne, to building the base of independence for persons with disabilities through supports for education and skills development.

Canadians of working age with disabilities tend to have lower incomes than persons without disabilities. A key reason is that individuals with disabilities generally have lower levels of both education and employment than other Canadians.

Data from the 2001 Participation and Activity Limitation Survey show that only 51 percent of persons with disabilities ages 25 to 54 were employed, compared with 82 percent of persons without disabilities. The survey also indicated that, for the same age group, 46 percent of persons with disabilities had post-secondary education, compared with 57 percent of those without disabilities.[1]

Canadians with disabilities are willing and able to make a positive contribution to society, and it is clearly in the national interest as well as their own that they be enabled to do so. In fact, the federal government recently embarked upon a National Strategy on Skills and Learning to ensure that all members of Canada's current and emerging workforce are highly skilled and adaptable.

International studies also stress the importance of employment and education. The Organisation for Economic Co-operation and Development, for example, has stated that investment in human capital is at the heart of strategies to promote economic prosperity, fuller employment and social cohesion.[2]

However, persons with disabilities often face barriers in pursuing employment or education that leads to employment and full participation. In some cases, employers and educational institutions provide the supports necessary to respond to the special needs of persons with disabilities. In other cases, however, persons with disabilities must acquire these supports on their own. Either way, they typically must pay for some or all of these costs.

---

[1] Human Resources Development Canada, *Disability in Canada: A 2001 Profile*, 2003, p. 23.

[2] Organisation for Economic Co-operation and Development, *Human Capital Investment: An International Comparison*, 1998, p. 7.

The government and the disability community have made the inclusion of persons with disabilities a key goal. To achieve this, it is essential that barriers to employment and education be reduced and eliminated, where possible. One of the Committee's priorities was to ensure that the tax system recognize the additional costs that persons with disabilities face when they seek to participate in the labour force and in educational institutions. Such recognition is essential if the tax system is to help remove barriers to work and enable persons with disabilities to make their full contribution to society and lead fulfilled lives.

In this chapter, we examine how the tax system recognizes the costs of accommodating persons with disabilities in education and employment. We begin with the personal income tax system where we discuss how tax relief is provided when the cost is covered by individuals themselves with their own resources or government assistance. We believe that the funds to help pay for these supports should not be taxed.

Given the importance of this issue, we made it one of our first areas of study. In fact, we put forward an interim recommendation in January 2004 that a deduction be provided for the cost of disability supports purchased by persons with disabilities in order to pursue employment or education. Such a deduction helps ensure horizontal equity by treating a person with disability expenses in a similar fashion to a person without a disability who has the same net income.

We consider this recommendation to be a crucial part of our package to ensure greater fairness and opportunity to persons with disabilities, and we were pleased that the government accepted our interim proposal in its 2004 budget.[3] This new measure and its proposed enhancements are described in more detail below.[4] A key feature of the deduction for disability supports is that it ensures that government assistance for students with disabilities to help them acquire disability supports for education is not subject to tax.

The Committee sought not only to improve tax recognition for the cost of disability supports, but also to improve the awareness of these measures. For example, many disability supports are recognized under the medical expense tax credit. But persons with disabilities and their caregivers may not seek tax relief under this measure because they are not aware that they can claim some disability-related expenses. We believe that changing the name of this credit to the 'medical and disability expense tax credit' would improve awareness, and we make a recommendation to that effect.

We also recommend that the Department of Finance and the Canada Revenue Agency gather research data on the medical expense tax credit. It has been the fastest-growing

[3]Department of Finance Canada, *The Budget Plan 2004*, 2004, pp. 103, 324–327.

[4]At the time of writing, legislation to enact the 2004 federal budget tax proposals had not been approved by Parliament.

tax measure delivering health-related tax relief to taxpayers, including persons with disabilities.

With respect to employment, a significant component of the federal tax system is the refundable medical expense supplement. The supplement provides some financial aid to low-income workers with above-average medical expenses, including persons with disabilities. The measure addresses, to a limited extent, the important issue of the loss of support from social assistance when persons with disabilities try to move off this income program to enter the workforce. As their income rises, they frequently lose their eligibility for income-tested disability supports and health benefits and end up paying for these items on their own. After reviewing the measure, we recommend that the supplement be enhanced to give more support to low-income workers with high medical expenses.

The Committee also reviewed the provisions for accommodating persons with disabilities within registered education savings plans. These plans provide tax-assisted savings to enable families to put aside money for post-secondary education for their children. In this chapter, we suggest improvements to the registered education savings plans rules to better reflect the special needs of students with disabilities.

We also reviewed the present tax incentive for employers relating to the cost of accommodating the special needs of persons with disabilities. Given the lack of awareness of these measures, we recommend that this information be publicized more broadly. New measures to stimulate the entry of persons with disabilities into the labour market by increasing the probability of their receiving required accommodation should be considered in the longer term.

We conclude this chapter by discussing the tax treatment of disability pension income that individuals receive when they have to leave the labour force because of disability. This discussion is in response to a request from the House of Commons Standing Committee on Human Resources Development and the Status of Persons with Disabilities, which recommended in its June 2003 report, *Listening to Canadians: A First View of the Future of the Canada Pension Plan Disability Program*, that we examine the taxation of Canada Pension Plan disability benefits.

Tax Treatment of Disability Supports

In some cases, employers will cover the costs of accommodating the needs of employees with disabilities. Generally, these benefits are non-taxable to the employee.

However, in many cases persons with disabilities themselves may have to purchase disability supports, such as sign language interpreters and talking textbooks, in order to overcome barriers to their participation in education or employment. Some pay for these supports from their own income, while others receive financial assistance from governments or other sources, such as private insurance companies.

A fair tax system attempts to ensure that individuals in similar circumstances pay similar amounts of tax. Current tax credits for persons with disabilities recognize that these individuals (and those who care for them) face additional disability-related expenses, thereby reducing their ability to pay tax.

Going further and recognizing these costs relating to securing employment and training through a deduction in the tax system would ensure that individuals who purchase disability supports for these purposes – either with government assistance or with their own income – pay no more tax than persons with the same net income (after disability costs) who do not need to purchase these supports. At the same time, however, these tax measures are not intended to reimburse individuals for costs they incur.

Until recently, persons with disabilities could receive limited tax relief for the cost of disability supports for employment and education only through the attendant care deduction or the medical expense tax credit.

Attendant Care Deduction
This deduction recognized the costs incurred by taxpayers eligible for the disability tax credit who required attendant care in order to earn business or employment income or to attend school. The attendant could not be a spouse or common-law partner and had to be 18 years of age or older.

The deduction was limited to the lesser of the qualifying amounts paid to the attendant and two-thirds of the taxpayer's earned income. For those attending school, the maximum deduction was two-thirds of the taxpayer's earned income plus two-thirds of the lesser of (a) the taxpayer's income from other sources (up to $15,000) and (b) $375 times the number of weeks of attendance at the designated educational institution or secondary school.

As discussed later in this chapter, as a result of an interim recommendation made by this Committee, the March 2004 federal budget proposed a disability supports deduction that will subsume and greatly expand the attendant care deduction.

Medical Expense Tax Credit
The medical expense tax credit recognizes the effect of above-average medical expenses on an individual's ability to pay tax. For 2004, the credit equals 16 percent of qualifying medical expenses in excess of the lesser of $1,813 and 3 percent of net income. The net

income threshold is used to determine above-average expenses. There is no upper limit on the amount of eligible expenses that may be claimed.

Many expenses that persons with disabilities incur for education or employment are eligible for the medical expense tax credit, including tutoring for persons with learning disabilities, sign language interpreter fees and talking textbooks.

This measure and the Committee's associated recommendations are discussed in greater detail later in the chapter.

Tax Relief for Students with Disabilities

Students with disabilities may also receive tax relief through the tuition and education credits as well as the $3,000 exemption for scholarship and bursary income.

In the case of the education credit, part-time students with disabilities can claim the full-time education amount ($400 per month) for each month of part-time study at a post-secondary educational institution or occupational training program certified by the Minister of Human Resources and Skills Development. Eligible students include those who qualify for the disability tax credit and those who cannot reasonably be expected to enrol full time because of a certified mental or physical impairment. In order to be eligible for the education credit, the student's program must be at least three weeks long and involve at least 12 hours of course work per month.

Issues with Tax Treatment

In reviewing these measures prior to making its interim recommendation, the Committee determined that they do not always provide full tax recognition of the cost of disability supports. This issue is of particular concern with respect to the medical expense tax credit:

- Given that only expenses in excess of the medical expense tax credit threshold are recognized (i.e., the lesser of 3 percent of net income and $1,813), the portion of expenses below the threshold does not qualify for relief.

- If grants used to purchase disability supports are included in net income, as they would be when tax recognition is provided under the medical expense tax credit, such inclusion may affect the receipt of income-tested benefits, such as the GST credit and the Canada Child Tax Benefit.

- Because the medical expense tax credit is a credit, it offsets tax owing at the lowest tax rate (i.e., 16 percent). It is thus worth the same amount to taxpayers in all tax brackets. The medical expense tax credit, however, does not completely offset the tax owing of higher-income taxpayers on the income used to purchase disability supports.

As a result, some persons with disabilities may pay tax on the income they use to purchase disability supports.

These shortcomings of the pre-2004 budget system underscore a related problem highlighted in some of the submissions to the Committee. The Prince Edward Island Association for Community Living, the Autism Society of Prince Edward Island, the Canadian Hearing Society, ARCH: A Legal Resource Centre for Persons with Disabilities and Disability Services of the University of Manitoba all raised the issue of the tax treatment of government assistance for disability supports. This concern was also identified by the Opportunities through Work and Rehabilitation Society in its submission to the Committee.

"It is unfair to tax students with disabilities on monies they receive to purchase disability supports, and results in a system where support is offered and then individuals are punished financially for having a disability and requiring the supports in the first place."
– Disability Services, University of Manitoba

Federal Government Assistance to Students with Disabilities

In addition to general assistance provided to students (e.g., Millennium Scholarships, Canada Student Loans), the federal government makes available two grants to financially assist post-secondary students with disabilities.

- The *Canada Study Grant for Students with Permanent Disabilities* is worth up to $8,000 and is intended to fund education expenses to accommodate the special needs of persons with disabilities such as tutoring, sign language interpreters and note takers.

- The *Canada Study Grant for High-Need Students with Permanent Disabilities* is intended for students with disabilities who demonstrate financial need. It is worth up to $2,000 and is intended to fund educational costs such as tuition, books and supplies, and living costs.

The 2004 federal budget introduced a change to the Canada Study Grant for High-Need Students with Permanent Disabilities. This grant will now be paid up front, meaning that the grant will be provided first, and student loans will be intended for financial needs in excess of the grant. The new up-front grant will be available to students with disabilities who qualify for student loans.

These grants are administered by provincial and territorial governments.

Generally, government assistance for education and occupational training received as a bursary, scholarship or employment benefit under Employment Insurance is included in income. This practice applies as well to bursaries that enable persons with disabilities to purchase supports for education (e.g., hire a sign language interpreter). Some grants paid from the federal Opportunities Fund, depending on their nature, may also be subject to income tax.[5]

The existing tax credits provide relief from this taxation, although there are cases where this relief is incomplete. Prior to the introduction of the disability supports deduction, the result was that many individuals who received government assistance to help with the cost of disability supports ended up paying some tax on this assistance. Even though individuals might get government assistance intended to cover the full cost of supports, these individuals still had to pay a portion of the expenses from their own pocket.

The Committee supports very strongly the principle of non-taxability of government assistance for disability supports. A direct cash transfer intended for the purchase of a technical aid or special service is not a payment like wages or other earnings; it is a transfer paid in respect of a disability support. When recipients must pay income tax on this cash benefit, its real value decreases even though the cost of the item or service for which it was intended remains the same.

Many of the organizations that raised this issue in their submissions suggested that the government exclude from taxation any benefits paid in respect of disability supports. The Committee recommended instead, prior to the 2004 federal budget, that disability supports purchased for purposes of employment or education be fully deductible, in a manner similar to that of attendant care expenses.

RECOMMENDATION 3.1

To recognize the cost of required accommodation for persons with disabilities, the Committee recommended prior to the March 2004 federal budget that:

The government introduce a disability supports deduction to allow the full deductibility of the cost of disability supports purchased for the purposes of employment or education.

The March 2004 budget implemented this proposal by introducing a disability supports deduction. The measure has an estimated cost of $15 million annually.

This deduction addresses the issue of taxability of disability supports. By allowing the full deduction of such costs, the funds used to purchase these items are excluded entirely

---

[5] Payments made from the Opportunities Fund to individuals with disabilities include wage subsidies, which are taxable like any other source of employment income.

from the computation of net income for tax purposes. This new measure ensures that persons with disabilities do not have to pay tax on the benefits (from whatever source) they use to purchase these supports, and that this income will not affect income-tested benefits (see example).

Example: Tax Treatment of Disability Expenses

Thomas is a student living in New Brunswick who has a taxable income of $17,000 (composed of scholarships and earnings from a part-time job). He has a severe hearing impairment and needs a sign language interpreter in order to attend university. He received an additional $5,000 from a Canada Study Grant for Students with Permanent Disabilities that he uses to purchase sign language interpretation services to go to class, giving him a total income of $22,000 subject to tax.

Prior to the introduction of the disability supports deduction, Thomas would have had only partial recognition of his sign language interpreter costs under the medical expense tax credit. As a result, he would have paid $170 (net) from his own pocket to cover the income tax liability on his $5,000 grant. If Thomas had been eligible for income-tested benefits, such as the GST credit, he might have had to pay even more since the amount of the credit would have been reduced as a result of the grant being treated entirely as personal income.

With the new disability supports deduction announced in the 2004 federal budget, Thomas will be able to deduct from his total income the full amount of the grant he received to pay for the sign language interpreter fees. Thomas' taxable income will remain $17,000, which means that he will pay no income tax on the government assistance he received in respect of the interpreter services and his eligibility for income-tested benefits will not be affected.

In addition, a deduction treats equally those persons who receive assistance for disability supports and those who do not. It recognizes the cost of disability supports for employment or education regardless of the source of income used to pay for them, and thus grants relief for those who must pay for such aids from their own resources.

The disability supports deduction recognizes disability expenses for purposes of employment and education more completely than its predecessor, the attendant care deduction. First, the disability supports deduction recognizes more eligible expenses than attendant care. Second, the disability supports deduction allows persons with disabilities to deduct expenses for disability supports, up to the taxpayer's total earned income. The attendant care deduction was limited to two-thirds of the taxpayer's earned income.

Finally, the attendant care deduction required that taxpayers be eligible for the disability tax credit to claim the deduction. The disability supports deduction, by contrast, requires only that the need for some eligible expenses be certified by a medical practitioner.

It is therefore available to all persons who require disability supports and not only to those eligible for the disability tax credit.

New Disability Supports Deduction

Following are the provisions of the disability supports deduction as stated in the 2004 federal budget.

Deduction limits

In the case of an employee, the deduction generally will be limited to the lesser of the amounts paid for eligible expenses and the taxpayer's earned income. A similar limit also applies to students, except that they can also claim the deduction against some other income, based on the length of their education program.

Eligible expenses

The disability supports deduction will recognize amounts paid for:
- Sign language interpretation services
- Real-time captioning services
- Teletypewriters and similar devices
- Devices to be used by blind individuals in the operation of a computer
- Optical scanners and similar devices
- Electronic speech synthesizers
- Note-taking services
- Voice recognition software
- Tutoring services
- Talking textbooks
- Attendant care.

The need for some of these supports must be certified by a medical practitioner. For more details, please see *The Budget Plan 2004*, pp. 324–326.

Unlike the attendant care deduction, individuals will not have to be eligible for the disability tax credit in order to claim expenses under the disability supports deduction.[6]

Expenses claimed under the disability supports deduction will not be claimable under the medical expense tax credit. Persons who purchase disability supports for purposes other than education or employment will still be able to claim them under the medical expense tax credit.

---

[6] Eligibility for the disability tax credit is one means to substantiate a claim for attendant care.

We were pleased that the government responded positively to our recommendation by proposing in the March 2004 budget to replace the attendant care deduction with a broader disability supports deduction that will recognize attendant care as well as other disability supports expenses incurred for education or employment purposes.

We view the new disability supports deduction as an important and strategic part of efforts to improve the fairness of the tax treatment of persons with disabilities and enable their participation in the labour market.

Expansion of Eligible Expenses

While the Committee applauds the government's initiative in this area, we believe that some key disability supports have been overlooked. We consider that the proposed deduction could be improved further by including more disability-related expenses.

The Committee considered recommending the addition of an extensive list of expenses for the purposes of this deduction. This expansion could have been achieved either by adding specific expenses to the current list eligible for the deduction or by replacing this list with broad categories of expenses (e.g., personal supports and computer access technology), with a set of examples for each category. Under the latter approach, examples would be used for illustrative purposes only, and the principles would be inclusiveness and openness to emerging services and devices.

Due to cost considerations, however, we decided to focus initially on adding specific disability supports that are used strictly for the purposes of employment and education. Examples of expenses that we recommend be added to the current list include personal supports, such as job coaches and readers, and technical devices such as Braille note takers, page turners, print readers, voice-operated software, memory books and assistive devices used to access computer technology.

Going forward, the government should consider adding to the list of expenses eligible for the deduction other expenses that enable persons with disabilities to participate in education and employment. The objective would be to include all disability supports (personal supports, equipment and technical aids) designed specifically to assist the participation of persons with disabilities in employment and education.

RECOMMENDATION 3.2

To further improve the disability supports deduction, the Committee recommends that:

The cost of such items as job coaches and readers, Braille note takers, page turners, print readers, voice-operated software, memory books, assistive devices used to access computer technology, and similar disability-related expenses be added to the list of expenses recognized by the deduction.

We estimate that this improvement would cost $5 million annually.

As noted, the Committee favoured the principle of excluding support for disability aids from income. We were informed by the government that the only grants subject to income tax were those for employment and education. The introduction of the disability supports deduction puts in place a mechanism to ensure that government assistance used to pay for disability supports will no longer be taxed.

The Committee also felt strongly that persons with disabilities should be able to deduct from income the cost of disability supports used for education and workforce participation and paid for from their own resources.

With the introduction of the disability supports deduction, government assistance to purchase disability supports effectively will be non-taxable (i.e., the deduction offsets the inclusion in income of any assistance for disability supports). The Committee suggests that if, in future, cases are identified in which government assistance used for disability supports is subject to tax, the government should take immediate steps to rectify the situation.

Although government assistance in respect of supports should ultimately not be subject to tax, in some cases taxes may be withheld on grants. Even though under the new provisions such taxes ultimately will be refunded, the deduction of tax at source is inconsistent with the principle of non-taxability of disability supports.

When individuals are provided with funding for a disability support, initially they may receive less than the full amount of the grant. They are, in effect, being asked to shoulder part of the cost of the disability support until they fill in their tax return and receive a refund. This process can take months – which is particularly problematic for persons with disabilities who tend to have lower incomes.

The Committee feels that taxes should not be withheld at source on grants intended for disability supports that ultimately will not be subject to tax. This issue is complicated by the fact that a number of jurisdictions and different programs may be involved. The Canada Revenue Agency is currently examining the problem. The Committee suggests that if instances where taxes are being withheld on grants that are ultimately not included in net income are discovered, the government should remedy the situation.

Medical Expense Tax Credit

The medical expense tax credit (METC) recognizes the effect of above-average medical or disability-related expenses on the ability to pay tax.

Of all the tax measures delivering relief to persons with disabilities, the medical expense tax credit has been the fastest growing. The continual expansion and updating of the list of expenses eligible under the medical expense tax credit, together with growth in the use of prescription drugs and other health aids, mean that both the number of claimants and the cost of the measure have increased steadily over the past decade. As with almost all other tax measures, only a small percentage of claims for the medical expense tax credit is reviewed before they are allowed. This practice contrasts with claims for the disability tax credit, all of which are reviewed prior to being granted.

The number of taxpayers claiming the medical expense tax credit and who have expenses over the required threshold (the lesser of 3 percent of net income and a set dollar amount) has more than tripled since 1988 (see Figure 3.1).

Figure 3.1: Number of METC Claimants, 1988–2001
(with expenses over threshold)

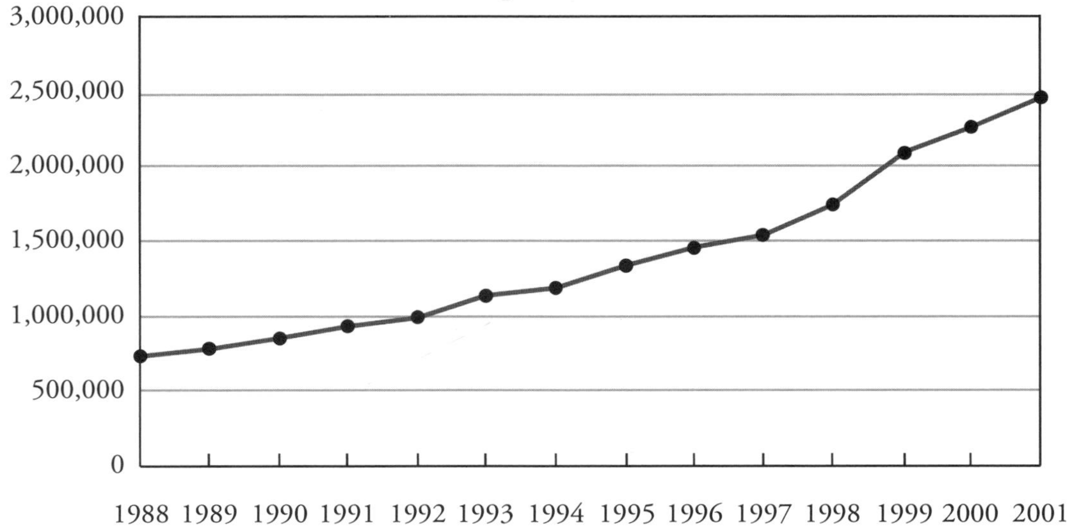

Source: Department of Finance

The medical expense tax credit provided $575 million in tax relief to Canadian taxpayers in 2001. As Figure 3.2 illustrates, the tax expenditure on the medical expense tax credit underwent an almost five-fold increase from 1988 to 2001. The Department of Finance projects that the amount of tax relief provided under the medical expense tax credit will increase to $765 million in 2004.

The medical expense tax credit provides relief to all taxpayers incurring above-average medical expenses. Although the credit may be claimed by anyone, it plays an important role in recognizing disability-related expenses, as many of the eligible expenses it recognizes are incurred by persons with disabilities.

Figure 3.2: METC Tax Expenditures, 1988–2001
(in millions of current dollars)[7]

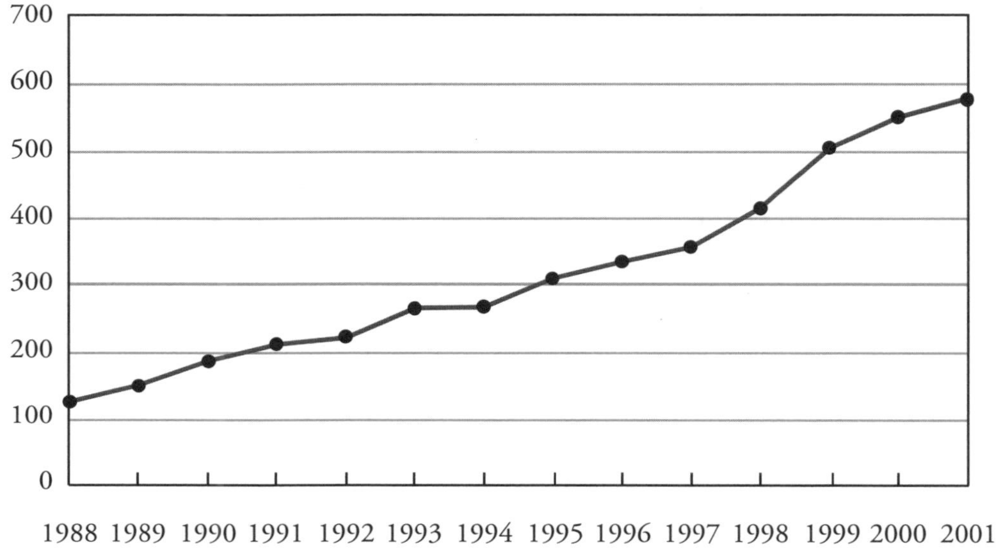

Source: Department of Finance

In 2001, the average medical expense tax credit claim for individuals and families making a claim for the disability tax credit was almost five times as high as the average claim for individuals and families with no claim for the disability tax credit (see Table 3.1). Further, individuals and families that had a disability tax credit claim were more than twice as likely to make a claim for the medical expense tax credit than individuals and families that had made no claim for the disability tax credit. This discrepancy was even larger for individuals and families with an individual eligible for the disability tax credit who was under age 65.

Nonetheless, families that had a disability tax credit claim comprised only about 5 percent of the total population of medical expense tax credit claimants.

---

[7] Tax expenditure data is presented in current dollars (i.e., not adjusted for inflation). When inflation is taken into account, the *real* tax expenditure grows, but at a slower pace.

Table 3.1: METC Claims by DTC Status and Age, 2001

	All Ages		< 65		65+	
	DTC	No DTC	DTC	No DTC	DTC	No DTC
Average METC claim	$1,123	$248	$682	$146	$1,568	$768
% with METC claim	33.0%	13.7%	28.0%	11.1%	38.1%	27.3%

Source: Department of Finance

It was brought to our attention that the federal government often characterizes the medical expense tax credit as a measure for persons with disabilities and includes this credit when estimating tax expenditures for persons with disabilities. The Committee objects to this characterization since the medical expense tax credit offers tax relief to all taxpayers, not only those with disabilities. We would therefore suggest stopping the practice of including the medical expense tax credit when calculating tax expenditures for persons with disabilities.

While the disability supports deduction addresses many of the shortcomings of the medical expense tax credit from the perspective of students and workers with disabilities, there is still one outstanding issue. A number of persons with disabilities and their caregivers are unaware that they can claim many disability-related expenses under the medical expense tax credit. Indeed, many of the expenses recently added to the list eligible for the medical expense tax credit would be incurred only by persons with disabilities or their caregivers.

"The Canadian Hearing Society supports the long standing position of other disability groups, [...] in the view that the Medical Expense Tax Credit should be renamed the Medical and Disability Expense Tax Credit [...]" – Canadian Hearing Society

We agree with the submissions to our Committee on the issue of awareness of the credit. We believe that changing the name of the credit will result in greater awareness of the availability of the medical expense tax credit to recognize certain disability-related costs.

RECOMMENDATION 3.3

The Committee recommends that:

The government change the name of the medical expense tax credit to the 'medical and disability expense tax credit.'

There is no cost associated with this recommendation.

The medical expense tax credit recognizes both above-average medical expenses and disability-related expenses. The Committee has found that generally there is little data available on the actual expenses claimed under this credit. This is a concern, particularly since the medical expense tax credit has been the fastest-growing tax measure that provides relief to persons with disabilities, among others.

The design of the present credit is also a subject of some question. Only expenses in excess of the lesser of 3 percent of income and $1,813 are claimable for the credit. However, expenses can be claimed by a spouse or common-law partner (with a lower, but taxable, income) so as to maximize the claim.

It is important to have reliable information about the medical expense tax credit in order to undertake periodic reviews of the measure, and the Committee believes that such data should be gathered. More specifically, there are concerns as to whether the expenses claimable under this provision include some costs that may be considered personal or optional, such as non-essential elective cosmetic surgery, designer eyeglasses, rejuvenation or spa treatments, and similar items.

RECOMMENDATION 3.4

The Committee recommends that:

The Department of Finance and the Canada Revenue Agency review currently available data and, where possible, gather new data on the actual expenses being claimed under the medical expense tax credit, and consider the appropriateness of these claims.

The estimated cost of this recommendation is nominal.

Refundable Medical Expense Supplement

The 1996 Federal Task Force on Disability Issues emphasized the need to reduce the disability-related costs that create barriers to the full participation of persons with disabilities. In response to the Task Force's recommendations, the government announced a number of measures in the 1997 federal budget.

One of the issues highlighted by the Task Force was that individuals might lose all medical- or disability-related supports provided by governments when they go off social assistance or other disability income programs, which can be a significant disincentive to enter the labour force. To address this issue, the 1997 federal budget introduced the refundable medical expense supplement.

For 2004, the maximum refundable medical expense supplement is 25 percent of the allowable portion of expenses that can be claimed under the medical expense tax credit plus 25 percent of the amount claimed under the disability supports deduction announced in the March 2004 federal budget, up to a maximum of $562.[8] To ensure that the supplement is targeted to persons entering or in the labour force, it is available only to workers with earnings from employment or self-employment above $2,809.[9]

Unlike most other credits, it is refundable – which means that individuals who do not have tax owing can benefit as well. If a worker's refundable medical expense supplement exceeds his or her net federal tax, the worker receives the difference. The refundable medical expense supplement is targeted toward those with low incomes, and is reduced by 5 percent of family income in excess of $21,301.[10]

The supplement benefited more than 300,000 Canadians in 2001 and is projected to provide $70 million in assistance in 2004. Table 3.2 shows that both the number of beneficiaries and the cost of the refundable medical expense supplement have increased steadily (approximately doubling) since its introduction in 1997.

Table 3.2: Number of Refundable Medical Expense Supplement Beneficiaries and Tax Expenditure, 1997–2001

Year	Number of Beneficiaries	Tax Expenditure (in millions of current dollars)
1997	165,000	23
1998	180,000	26
1999	225,000	36
2000	245,000	42
2001	315,000	55

Source: Department of Finance

Disability Tax Fairness

[8] The amount is indexed annually to the cost of living.

[9] The amount is indexed annually to the cost of living.

[10] The amount is indexed annually to the cost of living.

The Committee believes that the existing supplement has been a positive influence in enabling low-income Canadians with significant medical and disability costs to enter or re-enter the labour force. We also feel that an enrichment of this credit would further benefit many low-income workers and, more generally, Canadian society by encouraging workforce participation where possible.

The existing supplement could be augmented by raising the percentage of allowable expenses on which the benefit is based, say from 25 percent to 35 percent. However, greater federal assistance for a portion of out-of-pocket medical and disability costs for low-income Canadians could raise questions about appropriate federal and provincial roles with respect to the costs of health and disability supports.

Alternatively, the net family income threshold at which the supplement begins to be clawed back could be increased. But, in our view, the existing threshold seems high enough to cover the range at which individuals typically lose social assistance and other benefits.

The Committee considers that the best way to strengthen the existing credit is to increase the maximum claim, thus benefiting workers with substantial medical and disability costs, and without changing the overall structure of the program. Enhancing the maximum amount of the refundable medical expense supplement from $562 to $1,000 would allow these individuals to receive greater support (see example).

RECOMMENDATION 3.5

The Committee recommends that:

The maximum credit under the refundable medical expense supplement be increased from $562 to $1,000 and continue to be indexed to the cost of living.

The estimated cost of this recommendation is $20 million per year.

Example: Refundable Medical Expense Supplement

Melanie needs to purchase disability supports in order to mitigate the effects of her disability (these supports are required for everyday life, not necessarily for employment). The cost of these supports used to be covered by the provincial government when she was on social assistance. She recently began working at a job that pays $18,000 a year, but her employer does not provide a health plan that covers the cost of her supports. Melanie now has to pay for the supports herself, which cost $4,500 a year.

Currently, Melanie would receive the maximum $562 from the refundable medical expense supplement. She would also receive $634 in federal tax relief under the medical expense tax credit as well as some provincial tax relief. However, the significant amount of her disability-related expenses could cause her to consider giving up her job and going back on social assistance.

Increasing the maximum amount of the federal refundable medical expense supplement to $1,000 would allow Melanie to receive $990 from the refundable medical expense supplement, which is the full 25 percent of her expenses in excess of 3 percent of her income. This change represents a tangible improvement in her financial situation and helps ease the transition from social assistance to employment. She would continue to receive $634 in federal tax relief under the medical expense tax credit as well as some provincial tax relief.

Registered Education Savings Plans

Many students with disabilities receive help from their families to cover the cost of post-secondary education. The government provides a tax-assisted savings vehicle, known as registered education savings plans (RESPs), to help families save funds for the post-secondary education of designated children.

The rules for registered education savings plans allow a family to contribute up to $4,000 a year for a child, to a lifetime limit of $42,000 per child. Since 1998, through the Canada Education Savings Grant (CESG) program, the federal government has supplemented private savings in registered education savings plans: the first $2,000 contributed each year to a registered education savings plan for a child attracts a 20 percent Canada Education Savings Grant.[11] Generally, once the registered education savings plan is established, contributions can be made for 21 years and the plan generally must be wound up no later than the 25th year after it was established.

[11] The 2004 federal budget proposed enhancements to the Canada Education Savings Grant program to strengthen assistance for low- and middle-income families that wish to save for their children's post-secondary education. See Department of Finance Canada, *The Budget Plan 2004*, 2004, p. 118.

Contributions to registered education savings plans are not tax deductible. However, investment earnings on contributions can grow tax-free until they are distributed, at which point they are included in the recipient's income and taxed accordingly. In most cases, the recipient is a student whose total income (net of tuition and other claims) results in a minimal amount of tax.

Registered education savings plan funds can be withdrawn without penalty to pay for the costs of a full-time qualifying educational program. In order to qualify, an educational program must last at least three consecutive weeks, and must require a student to spend no less than 10 hours per week on courses or work in the program.

The program must be at the post-secondary school level. A post-secondary educational institution includes:

- a university, college or other designated educational institution in Canada;
- an educational institution in Canada certified by the Minister of Human Resources and Skills Development as offering non-credit courses that develop or improve skills in an occupation; and
- a university, college or other educational institution outside Canada that has courses at the post-secondary school level, as long as the student is enrolled in a course that lasts at least 13 consecutive weeks.

The registered education savings plan rules already include one special disability-related provision. Students with disabilities do not have to be registered full time at a qualifying post-secondary institution in order to benefit from a registered education savings plan.

However, students with disabilities often have special needs that must be accommodated in order to pursue post-secondary education. Doing so may involve additional costs, require access to a broader range of educational programs or require more time in order to begin or complete a post-secondary program. The Committee therefore recommends two measures to make registered education savings plans a more useful vehicle for the support of the education of students with disabilities. For the purposes of these measures, consideration must be given to defining the period of time that the child must be deemed to have a disability in order to qualify for these special treatments.

RECOMMENDATION 3.6

To address the special needs of students with disabilities, the Committee recommends that:

The time over which contributions may be made to a registered education savings plan for a person with a disability be extended to 25 years from 21 years, and that the time before the plans must be liquidated be extended from 25 to 30 years from inception.

The government broaden the list of educational programs that qualify under registered education savings plans to ensure that they accommodate the more diverse needs of persons with disabilities.

The estimated cost of these measures is nominal.

Business Income Tax Measures

The tax system provides additional recognition of capital expenses incurred by businesses to accommodate the special needs of persons with disabilities, whether as customers or employees. Usually, capital expenses such as purchasing a piece of equipment or making alterations to a building cannot be fully deducted from business income in the year these costs are incurred. Instead, these expenses are written off over a number of years under the Capital Cost Allowance system as the asset depreciates.

By contrast, the capital expenses to accommodate the special needs of persons with disabilities are fully deductible in the year they are incurred (see box for list).

Capital Expenses to Accommodate Persons with Disabilities That Are Fully Deductible

Eligible expenses include:
- renovations or alterations to a building to enable individuals with a mobility impairment to gain access to the building or to be mobile within it (e.g., the installation of interior and exterior ramps, hand-activated electric door openers and modifications to bathrooms, elevators or doorways);
- elevator car position indicators for individuals with a visual impairment;
- visual fire alarm indicators;
- listening devices for group meetings;
- telephone devices for individuals having a hearing impairment; and
- disability-specific computer software and hardware attachments.

Allowing full deductibility of these expenses encourages businesses to make these socially and economically important investments. The businesses receive in one year the tax relief they normally would get over many years, resulting in a reduction in the effective after-tax costs of their accommodation expenditures. However, decisions about investing in accommodation measures are not exclusively influenced by tax considerations.

Despite this favourable tax treatment, the Committee is concerned that it is not known whether businesses are taking advantage of these provisions in a significant way, perhaps due to lack of awareness. The Committee believes that steps should be taken by the Canada Revenue Agency to make businesses more aware of these provisions so that more investments are made to accommodate the special needs of persons with disabilities in the workplace and in the community.

RECOMMENDATION 3.7

The Committee recommends that:

Information for businesses about the deductibility of capital expenses to accommodate persons with disabilities be made more widely available in Canada Revenue Agency guides.

The estimated cost of this recommendation is nominal.

The Committee also considered whether any additional incentive should be offered to businesses to induce them to hire qualified persons with disabilities. Federal funding to encourage the employment of persons with disabilities is currently provided through the federal-provincial-territorial Multilateral Framework for Labour Market Agreements for Persons with Disabilities (a framework whereby the federal government grants funding to support employment assistance programming for persons with disabilities delivered by provincial governments) and the federal Opportunities Fund. Both the Opportunities Fund and some provincial programs pay wage subsidies.

We noted with interest the Work Opportunity Tax Credit in the U.S. tax system. This non-refundable credit is intended to increase the employment and earnings of workers belonging to certain disadvantaged groups that have consistently high unemployment rates by providing employers with an incentive to hire and retain these workers.

Persons with disabilities (defined as persons with a physical or mental disability that results in an impediment to employment) are one of the targeted groups. For their employer to be eligible for the credit, persons with disabilities must be referred to the employer upon completion of, or while receiving, rehabilitative services by a state employment security agency. The amount of tax relief that employers receive depends upon how long they retain the employees and the level of wages they pay.

The Work Opportunity Tax Credit is, in effect, a wage subsidy. Wage subsidies can be delivered either through the tax system (i.e., a credit like in the United States) or through a separate program as is done in Canada. Because the tax system is a blunt instrument, it may not be the most appropriate delivery mechanism for a wage subsidy. Unlike a focused program, the tax system cannot easily be tailored to individual circumstances.

For example, one concern with using the tax system is the fact that it is not well suited to handling complex eligibility criteria. The Work Opportunity Tax Credit addresses the question of eligibility by basing it on participation in rehabilitation service programs. In short, the tax credit relies on the eligibility criteria established by the rehabilitation programs.

The disability tax credit could act as a readily available eligibility screen for a similar tax incentive in Canada. Allowing only employees who are eligible for the disability tax credit to qualify for the purposes of such a credit, however, may be subject to some question. Although other eligibility criteria could be developed, this change would increase the complexity of the tax system.

The tax system also has more limited reach than other programs. Small and medium-sized businesses and the voluntary sector are important employers of persons with disabilities. However, if the wage subsidy were delivered through the tax system, many of these organizations might not benefit from the credit. Small and medium-sized businesses that do not have tax payable could not take advantage of the credit. Neither could charities and non-profit organizations, which are exempt from tax.

Despite these caveats, the Committee believes that a wage subsidy delivered through the tax system similar to the U.S. tax credit, under which employers would receive tax credits to offset the possibly higher costs involved in employing persons with disabilities, warrants investigation. More specifically, work is needed to determine whether such a measure would be a cost-effective way of providing an incentive to employers to consider the employment of additional persons with disabilities, and complement the proposed measures to enhance the ability of individuals to seek and fill such positions. To be cost-effective, such a program would need to adhere to a number of important conditions:

- Credits would be available only to employers who hire persons with disabilities for positions that do not displace other workers.

- Eligibility for the credit would require that the person with the disability be employed for a designated minimum length of time.

- The program would apply only to the hiring of persons with severe mental or physical disabilities, such as those currently eligible for the disability tax credit.

- The employer would have to provide appropriate standards of accessibility to the workplace.

- The program would have to fit in with existing government programs that provide wage subsidies and other types of employment and income supports for persons with disabilities.

RECOMMENDATION 3.8

The Committee recommends that:

As part of its efforts to develop measures to encourage the full participation of persons with disabilities, the government review the effectiveness of the United States' Work Opportunity Tax Credit.

Taxation of Canada Pension Plan Disability Benefits

The previous sections of this chapter focused on encouraging the entry into the labour force of persons with disabilities. Unfortunately, some individuals must leave the labour force because of a disability. Many of them then receive some degree of income replacement from private or public sources. This section discusses the tax treatment of this income.

Currently, disability benefits paid by the Canada Pension Plan (CPP)[12] are taxable, as is the case for retirement benefits under those plans. At the same time, tax relief is provided for employee contributions to the plans through a non-refundable tax credit. Tax relief is offered to employers through a deduction. Disability benefits under the CPP are payable only until age 65, when regular retirement benefits begin.

In 2003, the House of Commons Standing Committee on Human Resources Development and the Status of Persons with Disabilities identified its concern about the taxation of Canada Pension Plan disability benefits, particularly in light of the fact that some other forms of income replacement for individuals who leave the workforce because of a disability are not taxed. The Standing Committee recommended that our Committee examine how best to adjust CPP contributions deducted for tax purposes in order to remove amounts paid in respect of disability benefits and thereby eliminate the taxation of these benefits.[13]

---

[12] The province of Quebec operates its own similar plan, the Quebec Pension Plan. The tax treatment of contributions to and benefits from the Quebec Pension Plan is the same as that for the Canada Pension Plan.

[13] House of Commons Standing Committee on Human Resources Development and the Status of Persons with Disabilities, *Listening to Canadians: A First View of the Future of the Canada Pension Plan Disability Program*, 2003, p. 82.

There is a tax policy rationale for the current tax treatment of Canada Pension Plan disability benefits. CPP contributions are a work-related expense that reduces an employee's ability to pay tax as well as a legitimate business expense for employers. It is therefore appropriate to provide tax relief on these contributions.

At the same time, benefits from the Canada Pension Plan, like benefits from an employer pension plan or registered retirement savings plan (RRSP), are forms of earnings replacement that increase ability to pay tax and thus are treated like other forms of income. The tax treatment of the Canada Pension Plan is analogous to the tax treatment of employer pension plans and registered retirement savings plans: tax relief is provided on the contributions and withdrawals from the plans are taxed.

In effect, the tax on the contributions is deferred until money is withdrawn from the plan. (Further, the present treatment of CPP disability benefits is similar to private sector disability pension plans in which the employer pays part of the cost: the employers' contributions are deductible and the benefits are taxable.)

As noted by the Standing Committee, the current treatment of CPP disability benefits contrasts with some other forms of income replacement or support for persons with disabilities. For instance, two other forms of benefits – social assistance and workers' compensation – are non-taxable.

Social assistance payments are non-taxable because they are recognized as payments of last resort and since they are needs-tested, are already reduced as the individual earns income from other sources. Workers' compensation benefits have always been non-taxable because these programs were in place before the income tax was introduced. Making workers' compensation benefits taxable would require a major overhaul of their benefit and premium structure.

Under private sector insurance arrangements, disability benefits are paid under a variety of plans, subject to a range of conditions and terms. Where the employer contributes to the premiums for the plans, the payor generally obtains a tax deduction for the payment, but benefits paid under such arrangements are taxable.

Where the employer does not contribute to the cost of the plan, the employee obtains no tax relief for the premiums, but the benefits themselves are not included in income for tax purposes.[14] This practice is consistent with the principle noted above for the

---

[14]It should also be noted that where the employee pays the total cost of the disability benefits, the amount of benefits payable under the arrangement is frequently reduced from what would be a 'taxable equivalent' to take account of the fact that the benefits are not taxed.

Canada Pension Plan. If tax relief is provided for contributions, the benefits are taxable. When no tax relief is provided on the contributions, the benefits are not taxable.

The Standing Committee's suggestion to make Canada Pension Plan disability benefits non-taxable raises a number of complex issues. More specifically, such a change would depart from a position of tax equity, as non-taxable payments would be permitted from a plan where the contributions previously had been granted tax relief. Such treatment would be inconsistent with the general approach to tax-sheltered savings.

Even if the premiums for Canada Pension Plan disability coverage were not accorded tax relief, and the disability benefits were made non-taxable, there would be transitional issues. In the short term, individuals would be receiving non-taxable benefits based on contributions for which they received tax relief. Moreover, the non-taxation of benefits would provide little or no benefit to low-income persons with disabilities – as they are paying little tax – while it would allow higher benefits to Canada Pension Plan disability beneficiaries in higher-income tax brackets.

In addition, there is no basis to deny a deduction to employers for their contributions to the disability portion of the CPP. This issue might be resolved, at the cost of some complexity and huge transitional issues, by dividing the present CPP contributions between those related to disability and other benefits, and having the entire cost of the disability benefit paid for by the employee on a non-deductible basis.

Finally, making Canada Pension Plan disability benefits non-taxable may also require provincial consultations as this change might entail amendments to the Canada Pension Plan financing arrangements. While the Committee recognizes the concerns of the Standing Committee and the community on this issue, we are not able to recommend a general solution that would be preferable to the existing position.[15]

Interaction of Canada Pension Plan Disability Benefits and Private Insurance

Most private sector disability plans contain offset clauses, under which the full amount of benefits otherwise payable under such plans for disability is reduced by the amount of the disability benefits the recipient receives from the Canada Pension Plan. However, many private insurers are willing to pay the full amount of benefits (including what would be paid under the Canada Pension Plan) while the individual awaits approval of Canada Pension Plan disability benefits.

---

[15] For many individuals, the disability tax credit can largely offset the income tax owing with respect to Canada Pension Plan disability benefits. The Committee made a recommendation in Chapter 2 that could provide tax relief to more recipients of Canada Pension Plan disability benefits by increasing the take-up of the disability tax credit.

In these cases, there are 'assignment of benefit agreements' entered into by the claimant. Under these agreements, once Canada Pension Plan approval is obtained, the CPP will reimburse the private insurer for the equivalent of the Canada Pension Plan disability benefits it paid to the recipient prior to the CPP approval. While this arrangement is intended to provide as much income replacement to individuals as quickly as possible upon leaving the workforce because of their disability, there are tax consequences that the Standing Committee and others such as the Canadian Life and Health Insurance Association have raised as a concern.[16]

As noted, unlike Canada Pension Plan benefits, many long-term disability benefits from private insurers are non-taxable. When the private benefits are replaced by the retroactive Canada Pension Plan benefits, the recipient must pay tax on the CPP benefits that were assigned to the insurer. This practice can create hardship for some recipients, as they unexpectedly may be called upon to pay tax on benefits that they have already received (and spent).

The Committee recognizes the importance of this issue raised by the Standing Committee. We note that in its response to the Standing Committee report, the government committed to work with private insurers to develop possible solutions to address this issue.[17] We urge the government to find ways to resolve this issue expeditiously.

Disability Tax Fairness

[16] House of Commons Standing Committee on Human Resources Development and the Status of Persons with Disabilities, *Listening to Canadians: A First View of the Future of the Canada Pension Plan Disability Program*, 2003, p. 82.

[17] Government of Canada, *Response to "Listening to Canadians: A First View of the Future of the Canada Pension Plan Disability Program,"* 2003, p. 32.

Chapter 4:
Measures for Caregivers and Children with Disabilities

Chapter 4: Measures for Caregivers and Children with Disabilities

Introduction

Steps to promote the inclusion of persons with disabilities, along with measures to encourage education and employment, should be the overarching goal of tax measures for persons with disabilities. But the fact remains that many persons with disabilities rely to varying degrees on family and friends for financial and other support. Within this group, there are two distinct situations to consider: caregivers providing support to an adult with a disability and families raising a child with a disability.

Many adults with disabilities require some form of assistance. Data from the 2001 Participation and Activity Limitation Survey found that an estimated 1.2 million individuals with disabilities ages 15 to 64 reported receiving help.[1]

Individuals providing care to adult family members play a vital role by enabling persons with disabilities and elderly Canadians to live in the community. Indeed, such informal assistance within families is a crucial part of the network of private and public assistance to those requiring support, providing personalized care in familiar surroundings and relieving governments of substantial public costs that might otherwise be incurred.

According to the 2002 General Social Survey, the vast majority of caregivers feel positively about their caregiving responsibilities.[2] The problem is that there can be negative consequences associated with caregiving, including reduced free time, more health problems and greater non-discretionary out-of-pocket expenses for caregivers.

With respect to financial costs, data from the 2002 General Social Survey show that more than one-third of caregivers under age 65 incurred extra expenses due to their caregiving duties, as did slightly less than 30 percent of senior caregivers.[3] Many caregivers face additional economic costs in the form of lost income and employer-provided benefits due to changes in their employment situation, such as quitting a job, retiring early or reducing their hours of work. Further, informal caregivers are not usually remunerated for their work.

The 2002 General Social Survey data reveal that approximately one-quarter (27 percent) of female caregivers ages 45 to 64 and 14 percent of male caregivers in the same age group reported a change of work patterns.[4] Approximately one out of every ten women and a slightly lower percentage of men lost income due to their care duties.[5]

---

[1] Statistics Canada, *Disability Supports in Canada, 2001 – Tables*, Catalogue no. 89-581-XIE, 2003, p. 20.

[2] Statistics Canada, General Social Survey, *Cycle 16: Caring for an aging society*, Catalogue no. 89-582-XIE, 2003, p. 13.

[3] Ibid., p. 14.

[4] Ibid., p. 15.

[5] Ibid., p. 16.

Families raising children with disabilities must also deal with many challenges not faced by other families. Data from the Participation and Activity Limitation Survey found that about one in four children with some form of activity limitation received help with everyday activities (including personal care) because of a condition or health problem.[6, 7] This survey also shows that households with children with disabilities had lower household income than households with children without disabilities.[8]

In this chapter, we examine how the personal income tax system recognizes the additional costs incurred by caregivers (of both adults and children with disabilities). But the allocation of funds to parents involves more than just recognizing the costs they incur in respect of disability. There is an important developmental dimension to the support for families with children. We divide this chapter into two sections in recognition of these two distinct purposes of assistance to caregivers – to help recognize the cost of disability and to provide some additional support for child development.

In the first section, we begin with a brief discussion of the role that the tax system plays in addressing caregiving costs. We then deal with the various complex tax measures intended for those who care for adults with disabilities.

The Committee considered the possibility of enhancing the credits that recognize the non-itemizable or hidden costs borne by caregivers. But we decided against this option because these credits include the caregivers of persons over age 65 who may or may not have an infirmity, and thus these credits are not well targeted to the caregivers of persons with disabilities – our priority. Further, providing tax relief for specific, itemizable expenses help ensure that tax relief is directed more towards those most in need of support. We do suggest, though, that the federal government simplify and consolidate, where possible, the various measures intended for caregivers.

With respect to the medical expense tax credit, which recognizes itemizable or specific disability-related costs incurred by caregivers for their dependants, we recommend that this measure be amended to allow those caring for a relative with a disability to claim more of these expenses.

While ensuring proper tax recognition of the costs incurred by caregivers is crucial, we also believe that it is important to enable caregivers to save money in order to provide a better quality of life for their dependant. We therefore recommend that changes be made to the current rollover provisions of registered retirement savings plans (RRSPs) and registered retirement income funds (RRIFs).

---

[6] Statistics Canada, *Children with disabilities and their families*, Catalogue no. 89-585-XIE, 2003, p. 7.

[7] In the Participation and Activity Limitation Survey, separate questionnaires were used for children up to age 14 and those ages 15 and over. While Statistics Canada provides information on those ages 15 to 24 in its public releases, the Committee feels it would be useful if the data could be disaggregated into categories of 15 to 19 and 20 to 24, for example.

[8] Statistics Canada, *Children with disabilities and their families*, Catalogue no. 89-585-XIE, 2003, p. 11.

The second section of this chapter deals with the tax provisions intended for families that care for children with disabilities. We strongly believe that the Child Disability Benefit is key to providing assistance to low- and modest-income families caring for a child with a disability, and we recommend that it be enhanced.

Measures for Caregivers of Adult Dependants

Tax Recognition of Caregiver Costs

Caregivers may face two types of financial costs: out-of-pocket expenses and reduced income due to loss of capacity to maintain full or stable employment. The tax system is limited in its ability to address these costs.

The purpose of the tax system is not to compensate or reimburse individuals for expenses that they incur or for foregone income. The function of the tax system is to recognize extra costs incurred by Canadians with particular circumstances that reduce their ability to pay tax.

Fairness in taxation requires that individuals in similar situations with similar incomes pay similar amounts of tax. Cost recognition for caregivers in the tax system, effected through tax credits intended for caregivers, ensures that individuals who incur out-of-pocket expenses for the care of their dependants pay no more tax than individuals who do not incur these costs but have the same net income.

However, the tax system represents a blunt instrument for delivering relief to caregivers. The tax system is efficient in cases where the target population is easily identifiable – e.g., eligibility is based on level of income or age or number of children. It is also effective when all members of a given population face roughly the same costs related to similar conditions.

But the tax system is not the most appropriate delivery mechanism when the population is not easily identified or faces varying costs. With respect to eligibility, there is no simple and obvious characteristic to ascertain the status of caregiver. Moreover, persons with disabilities and seniors represent a heterogeneous population, with widely differing needs and associated costs, which means that caregivers also incur highly variable costs.

In cases where costs are not easily quantified, the tax system provides only a flat amount of relief to individuals who meet certain criteria. It thereby plays only a limited role in addressing these costs.

A substantial number of caregivers provide support and care to adult dependants with infirmities or to elderly parents and grandparents. Data from the Participation and Activity Limitation Survey reveal that, among adults with disabilities ages 15 to 64 who reported receiving help, 73 percent received this help from family living with them, 38 percent from family not living with them and 27 percent from friends or neighbours (respondents could choose more than one answer).[9]

The personal income tax system includes measures that recognize both itemizable and non-itemizable costs. Credits recognizing itemizable costs require taxpayers to list the specific non-discretionary costs that they must incur (referred to as 'itemization'). For example, the medical expense tax credit allows claims for specific extraordinary health costs, including those related to disabilities. To claim this credit, individuals must list the eligible expenses they incurred. Such an approach maximizes fairness by ensuring that tax relief corresponds to actual expenses.

In many cases and for certain types of expenses, however, this itemization can be administratively complex or impractical. Asking caregivers to list additional transportation costs or the marginal costs of housing paid on behalf of their dependants, for instance, would not be realistic. In these cases, the tax system offers recognition of non-itemizable (or general) costs. Individuals who meet certain criteria can apply for a flat amount of tax relief, regardless of actual expenses. The caregiver credit is an example of such a measure.

Caregivers providing care to adult dependants currently receive tax relief in recognition of non-discretionary costs through both non-itemizable measures for general costs and an itemizable measure, the medical expense tax credit, for specific disability-related costs. We review both types of measures in turn.

Measures for Non-Itemizable Costs

The personal income tax system currently includes three measures that offer tax relief to a broad range of individuals supporting or providing care to a dependent relative.

In addition to these measures, and as noted in Chapter 2, if individuals do not have sufficient federal tax owing to take advantage of the tax relief offered by the disability tax credit, they can transfer the portion of the credit that they cannot use to a supporting person. Caregivers supporting low-income persons eligible for the disability tax credit can thereby receive tax relief, which recognizes the disability-related expenses they incur on behalf of their dependants.

[9] Statistics Canada, *Disability Supports in Canada, 2001 – Tables*, Catalogue no. 89-581-XIE, 2003, p. 20.

a. Caregiver credit

The caregiver credit gives tax relief to individuals providing in-home care for an adult dependent relative with an infirmity, or a parent or grandparent age 65 and over. For 2004, the maximum credit amount is $3,784 for such a dependant, which results in a federal tax reduction of up to $605 (16 percent of $3,784).[10] The credit amount is reduced dollar for dollar when the dependant's net income exceeds $12,921 and is fully phased out when the dependant's net income reaches $16,705.

The caregiver credit was claimed by almost 120,000 Canadians in 2001, the latest year for which data are available. The credit is projected to provide $65 million in tax relief in 2004.

b. Infirm dependant credit

The infirm dependant credit affords tax relief to individuals providing support to an adult dependent relative with an infirmity. The dependant may live in a separate residence.

For 2004, the maximum credit amount is $3,784, which gives a federal tax reduction of up to $605 (16 percent of $3,784). The credit amount is reduced dollar for dollar when the dependant's net income exceeds $5,368 and is fully phased out when it reaches $9,152. (As noted below, some supporting persons may have a choice as to whether to claim the infirm dependant credit or the caregiver credit, but cannot claim both.)

Close to 15,000 individuals claimed the infirm dependant credit in 2001. It is projected that this tax measure will provide $5 million in tax relief in 2004.

c. Eligible dependant credit

The eligible dependant credit gives tax relief to individuals providing in-home support to a parent, a grandparent, an adult brother or sister with an infirmity or a dependent child under 18.[11] The dependant must reside with the supporting taxpayer, and must be wholly dependent for support upon that person at some time during the year.

For 2004, the maximum credit amount is $6,803, resulting in a federal tax reduction of up to $1,088. The credit is reduced when the dependant's net income exceeds $681 and is fully phased out when the dependant's net income reaches $7,484.

The eligible dependant credit can be claimed only by individuals who are single, separated, divorced or widowed. Persons who are married or have a common-law partner cannot claim the eligible dependant credit. The purpose of the credit is to recognize that a

---

[10] Additional credits are provided by the provinces and territories. All amounts noted are indexed to the cost of living.

[11] The eligible dependant credit was formerly referred to as the equivalent-to-spouse credit.

taxpayer without a spouse who is supporting a dependent child, parent or grandparent is less able to pay tax than a similar person with the same income and no such dependant.

As the eligible dependant credit may be used with respect to both dependants with and without infirmities, the breakdown of individuals claiming this credit for an adult relative with an infirmity is not available.

Table 4.1: Value of Credit Amounts and Income Thresholds
2004 Taxation Year (dollars)

	Caregiver Credit	Infirm Dependant Credit	Eligible Dependant Credit
Credit amount	3,784	3,784	6,803
Income threshold	12,921	5,368	681
Income level where credit is phased out	16,705	9,152	7,484
Maximum amount of tax relief available (16% of credit amount)	605	605	1,088

Source: Department of Finance

A key concern expressed by the disability community is the complexity of the different tax measures available to those caring for adult dependants and the lack of clarity in terms of who can claim the credit. Each of the caregiver measures discussed above has unique eligibility requirements and different income thresholds. Moreover, there are complex interactions between these credits (see box).

Committee members also pointed out that there are no definitions of the terms 'support' and 'infirmity' in the law (important concepts where tax measures for caregivers are concerned), which adds to the confusion. In addition, the conditions for determining when a person is dependent on a taxpayer vary from credit to credit – e.g., the requirement for the taxpayer and the dependant to reside together or the age of the dependant. Overall, the credits described in this section are not targeted specifically toward persons with disabilities – the Committee's main focus.

It is not clear that this degree of complexity is required. It has led to a lack of understanding on the part of taxpayers that can negatively affect the take-up rate. We considered some approaches that might simplify and consolidate the different measures, but noted that any new and simpler measure likely would reduce benefits for some. An alternative could be designed so that no one would lose tax recognition, but it would involve substantial fiscal costs.

Interactions Between Credits

Taxpayers who are married or in a common-law relationship may apply for the caregiver credit or the infirm dependant credit with respect to a dependant other than their spouse or partner. Taxpayers who claim the caregiver credit for a dependant cannot claim the infirm dependant credit in respect of that dependant, nor can anyone else.

If more than one taxpayer is entitled to apply for the caregiver credit or the infirm dependant credit in respect of the same dependant, they can split the claim for that dependant. The total of their combined claim cannot be more than the maximum amount allowed for that dependant.

Taxpayers who are single, separated, divorced or widowed, and support an adult brother or sister living with them who is dependent by reason of mental or physical infirmity may request the eligible dependant credit. Taxpayers who claim the eligible dependant credit may not claim the infirm dependant credit or the caregiver credit. However, they may apply for an additional amount in cases where the value of the caregiver credit or the infirm dependant credit, had they been able to claim it, would have exceeded the value of the eligible dependant credit. In these cases, they may claim an additional amount equal to the value by which the caregiver credit or the infirm dependant credit (whichever is appropriate) exceeds the eligible dependant credit.

Any of these claims can be combined with a claim for a transfer of the disability tax credit from the dependant, if applicable.

Despite these difficulties, we believe that it would be worthwhile to examine the caregiver credit, the infirm dependant credit and the eligible dependant credit to consider whether simplification, and even consolidation, of the credits might be possible, perhaps over time.

The Committee also considered recommending an increase to these three measures for caregivers. The amount of the caregiver credit and the infirm dependant credit is $3,784 in 2004. This amount recognizes 'everyday' out-of-pocket expenses, such as transportation, non-prescription medications and homemaking supplies, incurred over the course of a year for the care of dependants. Clearly, some caregivers incur expenses that far exceed that amount.

However, not all caregivers have out-of-pocket expenses associated with their caregiving responsibilities. The 2002 General Social Survey found that only about one-third of family members and friends who provide care to seniors with a long-term health problem incur extra expenses.[12] Further, the results of a recent survey conducted for Health Canada, the *National Profile of Family Caregivers in Canada*, suggest that only a small proportion of caregivers pay annual out-of-pocket expenses that exceed the current caregiver and infirm dependant credit amount.[13] In addition, caregivers can receive tax relief from the disability tax credit (which also recognizes non-itemizable costs) as a transfer from their dependant.

Based on available data, it appears that, in general, the current amounts of credits for caregivers provide appropriate tax recognition of everyday out-of-pocket expenses for most households. We recognize that, in particular circumstances, the expenses incurred by caregivers can significantly exceed these amounts. Nevertheless, the Committee decided that, on tax policy grounds, there were no clear reasons for increasing the amount of the general caregiver measures discussed above. We were particularly concerned, as noted, that the increases would not necessarily be directed towards persons caring for individuals with disabilities.

Measure for Itemizable Costs

a. Medical expense tax credit

In many cases, caregivers incur disability-related and medical expenses, in addition to basic living expenses, for a dependent relative. The medical expense tax credit recognizes the effect of itemizable (or specific) above-average medical or disability-related expenses on an individual's ability to pay tax.

For 2004, the credit equals 16 percent of qualifying medical expenses in excess of the lesser of $1,813 and 3 percent of net income. The net income threshold is used to determine above-average expenses. Taxpayers may claim the medical expenses incurred by themselves and their spouses.

The treatment of expenses paid by taxpayers on behalf of specified dependent relatives was improved in the 2004 federal budget. Prior to that time, the ability of taxpayers to claim expenses in respect of dependent relatives other than a spouse or a minor child was limited.

The 2004 federal budget proposed to allow caregivers to claim more of the medical and disability-related expenses they incur on behalf of dependent relatives. Specifically, for medical expenses paid on behalf of dependent relatives, such as a parent, grandparent, brother, sister, aunt, uncle, niece or nephew, taxpayers will be able to claim qualifying

[12] Statistics Canada, General Social Survey, *Cycle 16: Caring for an aging society*, Catalogue no. 89-582-XIE, 2003, p. 13.

[13] Decima Research Inc., *National Profile of Family Caregivers in Canada* – 2002, 2002, pp. 21–22.

medical expenses that exceed the lesser of 3 percent of the dependant's net income and $1,813.[14] The maximum eligible amount that can be claimed on behalf of dependent relatives will be $5,000.

This provision will ensure that caregivers receive fair recognition under the income tax system for medical and disability-related costs for dependent relatives. The Committee welcomes this measure.

We are concerned, however, that the maximum eligible amount that may be claimed on behalf of dependent relatives by caregivers under the medical expense tax credit is capped at $5,000 per year. While the limit is adequate for some, others will find that the eligible amount is restricted to less than their actual costs, especially for those caring for a dependant with a severe disability.

"Many persons requiring attendant care are dependent on approximately six hours of care in a 24-hour period at a rate approximately $13.33 per hour. This amounts to over $28,000 per annum..." – Canadian Paraplegic Association

The Committee therefore recommends an increase in the amount that can be claimed by caregivers with dependants eligible for the disability tax credit.

RECOMMENDATION 4.1

The Committee recommends that:

The limit of expenses claimable under the medical expense tax credit by caregivers be increased from $5,000 to $10,000 for those with dependent relatives eligible for the disability tax credit.

The estimated cost of this measure is $5 million annually.

Increasing the maximum eligible amount would allow caregivers to claim even more of the medical and disability-related expenses they incur on behalf of dependent relatives, as illustrated on page 97.

---

[14] Medical expense claims made on behalf of minor children are pooled with the medical expenses of the taxpayer and his or her spouse or common-law partner, subject to the taxpayer's minimum expense threshold (the lesser of 3 percent of the taxpayer's net income and $1,813), without, as proposed in the 2004 federal budget, regard to the income of the minor child.

Tax Recognition of Medical Expenses Paid by Caregivers

Diane provides support to her adult son, Patrick, who is eligible for the disability tax credit. Patrick has a part-time job and earns $10,000 annually. Diane pays all of Patrick's medical expenses, which are $8,000 a year. Diane currently has a net income of $50,000.

Under the measure introduced in the 2004 federal budget, Diane would be able to claim the portion of Patrick's medical expenses that exceed 3 percent of Patrick's net income, up to a maximum of $5,000. The $5,000 limit would prevent Diane from claiming all of the expenses in excess of Patrick's 3 percent threshold. She would claim $5,000 in expenses, for a federal income tax reduction of $800 ($5,000 x 16%).

Medical expenses incurred on behalf of Patrick	$8,000
Less: 3% of Patrick's net income ($10,000 x 3%)	-300
Net medical expenses	$7,700

By increasing the limit from $5,000 to $10,000, Diane would be able to claim $7,700 in expenses, for a federal income tax reduction of $1,232 ($7,700 x 16%).

Rollover Rules for Registered Retirement Savings Plans and Registered Retirement Income Funds

Caregivers also need to plan for the future. One of the most important concerns for parents caring for children with severe disabilities is to ensure that they will be properly provided for during and after the lifetime of the parents.

"When we think about securing a good life for our family members with a disability, we must also think beyond our lifetime to the lifetime of our family member. In fact, one of our constant worries is 'What will happen to my son or daughter with a disability after I die?'"
– Planned Lifetime Advocacy Network (PLAN)

While there is no specific tax-assisted vehicle for disability-related savings, the tax system does include measures that support the use of tax-deferred savings for this purpose. Persons with disabilities and their families, like all Canadians, are able to benefit from the deferral of tax on contributions to registered retirement savings plans (RRSPs), which encourages and assists Canadians to save for retirement. Contributions to these plans are deductible from income. The investment income is not taxed as it accrues and all withdrawals and benefit payments are included in income and taxed at regular rates.

When the annuitant (or owner) under an RRSP or a registered retirement income fund (RRIF)[15] dies, the value of the RRSP or RRIF is generally included in computing the deceased's income for the year of death. However, preferential tax treatment on RRSP or RRIF distributions made after death is provided in certain cases. These include the distribution of proceeds to a child or grandchild who was financially dependent on the deceased annuitant by reason of physical or mental infirmity. In this case, the proceeds from the registered retirement savings plan or registered retirement income fund may be transferred without tax to the registered retirement savings plan of the child or may be used to purchase an immediate life annuity.

For 2004, a child or grandchild is considered to be financially dependent if the child's income for the year preceding the year of death was below $14,035. This threshold is indexed to inflation.

In its submission to the Committee, the Planned Lifetime Advocacy Network (PLAN) proposed a number of changes to the current provisions regarding the rollover of registered retirement savings plans and registered retirement income funds to a dependant with a disability.

We carefully examined these and similar proposals. While some of them might allow significantly greater flexibility in providing support through registered retirement savings plans to dependants with disabilities, the Committee wanted to ensure that favourable tax treatment be limited to those cases where the plan was intended exclusively for the benefit of persons with disabilities. The main issue is the desire to introduce discretion with respect to annual distributions to persons with disabilities who might be the beneficiary of a registered retirement savings plan.

Given that it is difficult to forecast the needs and circumstances of persons with disabilities many years in advance, such discretion will prove to be helpful in matching payouts to actual current requirements. It may also provide an opportunity to govern distributions to or for persons with disabilities to ensure that they continue to qualify for social assistance and other public programs. However, such discretion may also enable individuals without disabilities to benefit from the tax deferral.

Balancing all of these concerns, we believe that some additional flexibility in dealing with registered plans that are to provide benefits to persons with disabilities would be justified, with appropriate safeguards.

---

[15] Individuals are required to convert an RRSP to a RRIF or purchase an annuity with their RRSP savings by the end of the year they turn age 69. Although contributions to RRIFs are not permitted, the investment income continues to accrue on a tax-deferred basis. However, minimum RRIF withdrawals must start the year following conversion from an RRSP. The purpose of these rules is to ensure that savings in RRSPs are used to generate income in retirement, consistent with the basic purpose of the tax deferral.

RECOMMENDATION 4.2

The Committee recommends that:

The government review the RRSP/RRIF rules in order to allow additional flexibility in respect of a deceased's RRSP or RRIF proceeds left to a financially dependent child or grandchild with a disability. Such provisions should include allowing these proceeds to be rolled over to a discretionary trust for that individual, provided that no person other than the disabled beneficiary may access the income or capital of the trust during his or her lifetime.

The revenue cost of this measure is small.

In our discussions, the Committee also noted that the establishment of tax pre-paid savings plans has been suggested by a number of tax policy experts. If such a program were set up, families may be able to use such plans to provide an additional long-term support to their children with disabilities.

A tax pre-paid savings plan involves establishing registered savings vehicles where the contributions are not deductible for tax purposes, the annual income of the plan is exempt from tax and distributions from the plan are not included in the tax base. The Committee suggests that if the government proceeds with introduction of such a plan, the position of dependants with disabilities should receive specific consideration.

Measures for Children with Disabilities

According to the 2001 Participation and Activity Limitation Survey, an estimated 155,000 children between ages 5 and 14 who were living in households had activity limitations in that year. This number represents about 4 percent of all children in this age group. Of these children, about 89,000, or 57 percent, experienced mild to moderate disabilities, while the remaining 66,000, or 43 percent, experienced severe to very severe disabilities.[16]

Most parents or guardians who have children with disabilities face additional challenges. The extra cost of raising a child with a disability can cause financial hardship. The needs of the child often force one parent to quit work or seek a part-time or less demanding job. Like most families, these parents want to ensure that they can provide developmental opportunities that are available to other children.

There are three tax-based measures for families caring for children eligible for the disability tax credit that recognize the financial burden of families. The first two are

---

[16] Statistics Canada, *Children with disabilities and their families,* Catalogue no. 89-585-XIE, 2003, p. 6.

measures that recognize the higher costs of raising a child with a disability and the third is a supplement to the Canada Child Tax Benefit, a benefit delivered through the tax system. The Committee felt that the latter also recognizes the need to help families provide for the development of their children.

Disability Tax Credit Supplement for Children

The disability tax credit has a supplement for children, which affords additional tax relief for children with severe and prolonged disabilities who qualify for the disability tax credit.

For 2004, the supplement provides an additional federal tax reduction of up to $605 or 16 percent of $3,784. To target this extra relief to families providing unpaid care, the $3,784 supplement amount is reduced dollar for dollar by the amount of child care expenses or attendant care expenses claimed under the medical expense tax credit over $2,216.

The number of tax filers claiming the disability tax credit supplement for children is not available, as it is combined with all other taxpayers claiming the disability tax credit. Similarly, the tax expenditure on the disability tax credit includes the disability tax credit supplement for children.

Child Care Expense Deduction

The child care expense deduction recognizes the child care costs incurred by single parents and two-earner families in the course of earning business or employment income, pursuing education or performing research. The child care costs of couples may also be recognized when one or both parents are pursuing education, or when one parent is incapable of caring for children due to a mental or physical infirmity. The infirmity needs to be certified in writing by a medical doctor.

In general, the child care expense deduction may be claimed in respect of children under age 16, with a limit of $7,000 for care of children under age 7 and $4,000 for children over age 7. However, child care expenses may be claimed for a child of any age if that child is dependent by reason of mental or physical infirmity (including being eligible for the disability tax credit). In addition, the child care expense deduction limit is more generous in respect of children who qualify for the disability tax credit ($10,000, regardless of age).

Child Disability Benefit

The main federal instrument for providing financial assistance to families with children is the Canada Child Tax Benefit, an income-tested benefit delivered through the tax system. The Canada Child Tax Benefit (CCTB) has two main components: the CCTB base benefit, which assists low- and middle-income families, and the National Child Benefit supplement, which provides additional assistance to low-income families.

Both the CCTB base benefit and the National Child Benefit supplement are income-tested based on family net income.

The Canada Child Tax Benefit has a supplement, the Child Disability Benefit, which was introduced in the 2003 federal budget. It is paid to families on behalf of children who are eligible for the disability tax credit. The benefit helps recognize the special needs of low- and modest-income families with a child with a disability. For the July 2004 to June 2005 benefit year, eligible recipients receive their annual Child Disability Benefit entitlement of up to $1,653 per qualified child as part of their monthly Canada Child Tax Benefit. The full $1,653 Child Disability Benefit is paid for each eligible child to families with net income below the amount at which the National Child Benefit supplement is fully phased out – $35,000 in July 2004 for families with three or fewer children.

Beyond that income level, the Child Disability Benefit is reduced. It phases out entirely when net family income reaches $48,549 for a family caring for one child with a disability, $49,564 for a family caring for two children with disabilities and $50,258 for a family caring for three children with disabilities.

The 2003 federal budget projected that the Child Disability Benefit would assist 40,000 families and cost $50 million per year.

The Committee strongly believes in the importance of providing a benefit to low- and modest-income families with children with disabilities. There are improvements that can be made to the current design.

First, there is room to increase the amount of the Child Disability Benefit to help families defray additional disability-related costs. Raising the amount of the benefit would deliver extra help to families caring for children with severe disabilities. The federal government would have to work with provinces and territories to ensure that any increase in the Child Disability Benefit would not reduce social assistance or other income-tested benefits.

Second, some families caring for a child with a disability are not eligible for the Child Disability Benefit. Because of its relatively low phase-out ($48,549 in 2004 for a family caring for one child eligible for the disability tax credit), only a few middle-income families and no higher-income families receive the benefit.

The Committee considered recommending that the Child Disability Benefit be paid to families with incomes above the current phase-out level – $48,549 of income in 2004 for a family caring for one child eligible for the disability tax credit. For example, the Child Disability Benefit could be extended to the same phase-out point as the Canada Child Tax Benefit – approximately $95,000 of income.

The phase-out option would respond to a concern raised by middle-income families that currently receive a reduced benefit or none at all. This option would also harmonize the design of the Child Disability Benefit with the Canada Child Tax Benefit, which effectively acts as the delivery agent for the disability portion.

The Canada Child Tax Benefit is paid to most families to help with the costs of raising children. Because the Child Disability Benefit provides additional assistance for disability-related costs, its extension to all families caring for a child with a disability that currently receive the Canada Child Tax Benefit should be considered a longer-term goal. While offering greater income support to middle-income families caring for a child with a severe disability is important, the Committee decided, given fiscal constraints, not to make a formal recommendation in this regard.

The Committee identified another potential source of funds for this measure. We discussed the fact that if an enriched Child Disability Benefit were delivered to most eligible families, then the government could consider reducing or even eliminating the disability tax credit supplement for children. The funds made available through the potential elimination or reduction of the disability tax credit supplement for children could be redirected to the Child Disability Benefit.

However, the elimination of the disability tax credit supplement for children would mean that some higher-income families would lose a modest amount of tax relief. Because of their higher incomes, these families are not eligible for the Child Disability Benefit and they would lose the tax recognition they currently receive through the disability tax credit supplement for children. There would still be a need to provide tax recognition through the disability tax credit supplement for children. The Committee therefore decided not to make a recommendation in this regard.

With these considerations in mind, the Committee recommends that the Child Disability Benefit be enhanced.

RECOMMENDATION 4.3

The Committee recommends that:

The federal government increase the amount of the Child Disability Benefit by $600 to raise the total maximum annual benefit from $1,653 to $2,253, and that this amount continue to be indexed to the cost of living.

The estimated cost of this measure is $15 million annually.

Finally, we recognized in our discussions that tax-related measures for caregivers are only one component of a broader set of federal policy instruments. As will be discussed in the Future Directions chapter, in part the special needs of caregivers might be better met by programs outside of the tax system that provide supports and services at home and in the community.

Chapter 5:
Future Directions

Chapter 5: Future Directions

In the course of our work, the Committee acknowledged that many issues which were brought to our attention and discussed went beyond our direct mandate. Yet these issues, such as the conceptualization of disability, the concept and practice of accommodation, and the various forms of social assistance for offsetting disability costs, are all relevant to the tax issues we were considering. While we do not review in detail areas that fall outside the scope of our mandate, we feel that it is important to share some observations that may contribute to future work on disability and, more specifically, the achievement of equity.

Going Forward: How Best to Assist Persons with Disabilities

Limits of the Tax System

The Committee recognizes that the purpose of the disability-related tax measures is to ensure fairness and equity among all taxpayers. Tax measures in general are not intended to redress income inequalities or compensate for low income. It is therefore essential not to distort their basic purposes.

The previous chapters focused upon specific tax measures and proposed possible remedies to improve fairness within the tax system. As we reviewed these issues, however, we felt compelled to ask questions about fairness from the perspective of public expenditure and relatively scarce dollars.

In our view, limited public funds should be directed toward those who most need the assistance. Unfortunately, there are two groups that will not benefit from many tax measures because most do not pay income tax: those with very low incomes and Aboriginal Canadians on reserve. Moreover, the tax system is ill equipped to deal with the pressures that invariably will arise from the growing support needs of an aging population.

a. Low-income Canadians

Most of the tax provisions the Committee was asked to review are of little or no value to persons with disabilities who are too poor to pay income tax and who have no supporting relatives who have taxable income. Individuals must first have a taxable income in order to derive any benefit from the current measures.

As explained in the chapter on employment- and education-related tax measures, a substantial proportion of persons with disabilities experience difficulty participating in the paid labour market. They face a range of barriers that make it impossible to find or maintain employment.

Even those who are fortunate enough to work often earn very low wages. They get little or no benefit from various tax provisions even though they may be employed. Still others will never be able to sustain themselves fully, or at all, through paid work.

b. Aboriginal Canadians

Aboriginal Canadians living on reserve are another major group that does not benefit from most disability-related tax measures. Most do not pay income tax and many do not even file a tax return. This issue is described in a research paper commissioned by the Committee.[1]

Our interest arises from the fact that the incidence of disability among Aboriginal Canadians is much higher than among the non-Aboriginal population – the most recent data available from the Canadian Community Health Survey puts the incidence of disability among Aboriginal Canadians at 31 percent.[2] Fetal alcohol syndrome and fetal alcohol effect among Aboriginal children and adults are of particular concern. These conditions are linked to a wide range of impairments in physical and mental functions.

Aboriginal Canadians who live in the northern regions of the country face unique problems. The basic costs of living 'north of 60' are higher than other parts of Canada. In addition, Aboriginal Canadians with disabilities face considerable barriers to participation. Most buildings, including homes, schools, band offices, churches, arenas and meeting halls are inaccessible. There is a lack of recreational facilities, accessible transportation and services, such as attendant care, homemaker services or respite for caregivers.

Many individuals face the choice of staying in their community or leaving their home and family to seek supports and services in urban centres – in Yellowknife, Whitehorse or the south. But Aboriginal persons with disabilities who live in urban centres or off reserve also face significant barriers. They run into jurisdictional complexities, related both to their Aboriginal status and place of residence, which often prevent them from gaining access to the disability supports they require.

The Committee recognizes that neither the Department of Finance nor the Canada Revenue Agency has the mandate to address concerns related to the supply and delivery

[1] Valentine, *Exploring the Relationship Between the Tax System and Aboriginal Peoples with Disabilities*, 2003.

[2] The Canadian Community Health Survey data do not include information on Aboriginal people living on First Nations reserves and are not directly comparable to the data from the Participation and Activity Limitation Survey. For more information, see Government of Canada, *Advancing the Inclusion of Persons with Disabilities*, 2002, pp. 6–7.

of disability supports. Nor does this issue fall within the purview of the Technical Advisory Committee. But it does relate to our work in the following way.

Those who have access to disability supports through various provincial and territorial programs typically pay only a small amount, or nothing, for those goods and services. In effect, their costs of disability are partially or fully offset by virtue of the fact that the required supports are provided through such programs. Once again, limited public funds may be better spent, in our view, on bolstering the supply of disability supports rather than enhancing tax measures.

c. Seniors

The trends in data that the Committee examined as part of our review of the disability tax credit, in particular, found that 60 percent of those claiming the credit are elderly. Their share is expected to rise over the next few years with an aging population.

The number of Canadians age 65 and over will double from nearly 4 million in 2001 to almost 8 million by 2026.[3] Seniors will account for 21 percent of the population by 2026, compared with 13 percent in 2001.

While seniors are healthier and living longer than ever before, the fact remains that the incidence of disability rises with age. Data from the Participation and Activity Limitation Survey indicate that nearly half of older Canadians experience some form of functional limitation. The disability rate for Canadians age 65 and older is 41 percent; it jumps to 53 percent for those age 75 or older.[4]

These figures represent more than just a cost pressure for the disability tax credit. In our view, they speak more broadly to the need for governments to tackle more strategically and comprehensively the fact that growing numbers of the population will require assistance with the activities of daily living. Many will need some help in offsetting the costs they incur both directly and indirectly in respect of their marked restriction.

Given these limits of the tax system in assisting persons with disabilities and addressing the needs of an aging population, the Committee felt it was important to note that there are other forms of assistance to enable the participation of persons with disabilities. While it was not our task to examine in depth alternative mechanisms for public investment, we spent considerable time generally reviewing these options. Frequently, providing tax recognition is not the right way to go unless there is no alternative.

---

[3] Statistics Canada, *Projected Population, By Age Group and Sex, Canada, Provinces and Territories, July 1, 2000–2026, Annual (Persons)*, CANSIM table 052-0001, 2004.

[4] Human Resources Development Canada, *Disability in Canada: A 2001 Profile*, 2003, p. 51.

Other Forms of Assistance

a. Building inclusive communities

Inclusion is a key goal of the disability community. This goal involves making more people aware of the benefits of including all members of the community, enabling persons with disabilities and their families to best represent their own interests and ensuring that persons with disabilities receive the resources in an environment that best meets their individual needs in order to maximize their potential. Building inclusive communities requires investments to reduce barriers that prevent persons with disabilities from full participation in all aspects of society. One way to address disability-related needs is through a concerted focus on and investment in accommodation, as we discussed in Chapter 1. Funds could be directed toward a range of organizations including schools, training centres, post-secondary educational institutions, small and medium-sized enterprises, and municipalities to enable them to introduce various measures of accommodation.

This type of investment would open up opportunities to persons with disabilities. It would also enable the sharing of the costs of disability among various levels of government, organizations and communities. In fact, in its report *Advancing the Inclusion of Persons with Disabilities*, the federal government acknowledges that "governments, communities, families, volunteer organizations, learning institutions, the private sector and labour are all important partners in making progress on disability issues."[5]

b. Labour market initiatives

As discussed in Chapter 3, the low participation rate and the high unemployment rate of people with disabilities continue to be major issues.

This problem of substantially low activity in the labour market for people with disabilities has been highlighted for well over 20 years as a key issue that needs to be addressed. The community of persons with disabilities, as recently as March 2004 at the national meeting "Connecting People to Policy," strongly reinforced the need for a comprehensive labour market strategy for Canadians with disabilities.

As detailed in Chapter 3, there are some important tax provisions to support this participation. We recommend additional measures to facilitate the participation of people with disabilities into the work force. However, these measures will be fully effective only if there are significant supplementary delivery and support mechanisms that, when combined within an integrated package, result in the required comprehensive labour market strategy.

Disability Tax Fairness

[5] Government of Canada, *Advancing the Inclusion of Persons with Disabilities*, 2002, p. 3.

Key components of such a strategy would include policies and programs that provide long-term, targeted support to ensure: access to additional skills development; the elimination of economic disincentives; proactive involvement and investment from employers; an appropriate supply of employment-related disability supports; mainstream employment programs that are fully accessible to persons with disabilities; a climate which encourages individuals to take work-related risks and to experiment; flexibility in the various services and supports; and active consumer control and coordination of the major elements.

The Committee recognizes the critical need for a comprehensive, pan-Canadian labour market strategy that integrates the efforts of the Labour Market Development Agreements, the Multilateral Agreements on Employment Assistance for People with Disabilities and the Opportunities Fund, along with significant additional resources to fill gaps not covered by the coordination of these existing initiatives.

c. Disability supports
Perhaps the most important action that the government can take to assist persons with disabilities is to invest in the supply of disability supports. There is currently a bewildering array of programs involving disability supports and assistance provided through direct programs and services, which are generally the responsibility of provinces and territories. The federal government is responsible for the delivery of these supports to First Nations and Inuit communities.

Some provinces operate special programs for the provision of technical aids and equipment. Other jurisdictions do not have broad-based programs but provide assistive devices and equipment for certain conditions, such as cancer, kidney ailments or cystic fibrosis.

All provinces and territories make available services for care at home including attendant care, home nursing care, homemaker services and respite. Some jurisdictions operate separate programs for each service while others combine the delivery of home supports under one 'umbrella' that offers the entire range. Overall, the result is a patchwork of programs that delivers substantial assistance but still leaves major gaps in coverage.

For years, the disability community has identified problems with respect to the availability and cost of disability supports under these programs. The community has named disability supports as its primary concern and recently confirmed this priority in March 2004 at a national meeting "Connecting People to Policy." One mechanism that has been proposed by several national organizations to address this issue involves the creation of a federal-provincial-territorial disability supports initiative that could operate in a fashion similar to recent agreements on early childhood development. The proposed initiative would consolidate existing programs and promote the development of a comprehensive network of goods and services throughout the country. It would seek to expand the quantity of existing supports, reduce their cost to consumers, improve their quality and ensure their portability across sectors and regions.

There is precedent for this kind of collaborative initiative. For example, in September 2000, all governments supported the federal-provincial-territorial Agreement on Early Childhood Development Initiatives.[6] Provinces and territories agreed to make investments in four streams of early childhood development programs, levered by a federal contribution of $2.2 billion over five years. It is therefore possible to envisage a national collaboration program that would see all levels of government working together to commit more resources toward supports for persons with disabilities.

A variation of this broader option is to focus upon specific supports or populations, such as caregivers. In this case, expenditure could be directed, for example, toward respite supports for families caring for relatives with severe disabilities or day programs for young children with special needs.

d. Disability supports allowance

A third form of assistance is to modify the disability tax credit to enable it to provide assistance to those too poor to pay tax. This objective could be achieved by making the credit refundable for low-income Canadians so that persons with disabilities and with little or no net federal tax would be able to take advantage of the current disability tax credit. A refundable disability tax credit has been suggested by a number of groups in their submissions to the Committee, including the Planned Lifetime Advocacy Network, the Canadian Association of the Deaf, the Multiple Sclerosis Society of Canada, the Canadian Hearing Society and the Canadian Paraplegic Association.

"It is apparent that making the Disability Tax Credit refundable as opposed to non-refundable would better enable persons with disabilities to be reimbursed for their out of pocket expenses regardless of where their income comes from."
– Canadian Paraplegic Association

However, a refundable disability tax credit would deliver only a very modest level of assistance to those with incomes below the taxpaying threshold. This approach would change the objective of the disability tax credit, shifting it from a mechanism that promotes fairness among those who pay income tax to a measure that provides some assistance to offset the additional costs of disability.

Disability Tax Fairness

[6]Although the province of Quebec did not sign this agreement, it receives federal funding for this purpose.

At the same time, we recognize that there is a significant portion of low-income Canadians for whom the current disability tax credit is of no benefit because they pay no income tax and have no supporting relatives who can claim the credit, live in institutional settings or receive social assistance. Under current social assistance rules, there is a possibility that a refundable disability tax credit would simply be recovered by the provinces and territories, with little benefit accruing to the individual. If the credit were made refundable, it would therefore be essential to ensure that recipients would be permitted to keep the refundable disability tax credit.

Alternatively, the disability tax credit could be redesigned as an allowance or benefit paid to all persons with severe disabilities. They would still qualify on the basis of a screen, such as the one currently used to establish eligibility for the disability tax credit. This option has been proposed in a recent study of the disability income and tax systems in Quebec conducted by researchers at Laval University.[7]

The authors of that study have recommended a flat-rate, non-taxable benefit of $250 a month for all persons up to age 65 who qualify on the basis of a severe and prolonged disability. (The amount is equivalent to the special needs allowance currently paid in Quebec to persons with disabilities on long-term social assistance.)

The proposed benefit would begin to taper off when the recipient's net income (as opposed to family income) reached $53,500 (in 2003 dollars), the level at which several other income security payments in Quebec begin to decline. The benefit would be funded largely through the elimination of the provincial disability tax credit and benefits currently provided to different categories of persons with disabilities (e.g., Allowance for Handicapped Children and the Allowance for a Severely Limited Capacity for Employment).

The Committee recognizes that there are several possible ways to better address the needs of persons with disabilities through programs that provide a range of goods and services or through benefits that pay cash to enable the purchase of disability supports rather than through tax measures. We believe that the effective delivery of supports is at the heart of advancing the inclusion of persons with disabilities and that a good balance between tax policy measures and social policy measures is required.

---

[7] Blais, Gardner and Lareau, *Un système de compensation plus équitable pour les personnes handicapées*, Office des personnes handicapées du Québec, 2004.

RECOMMENDATION 5.1

Our previous recommendations represent priority actions to improve tax fairness for persons with disabilities. Going forward, the Committee recommends that:

Priority should be given to expenditure programs rather than tax measures to target new funding where the need is greatest. The Committee recognizes that the development of such programs would involve consultations with provincial and territorial governments and the disability community.

In order for existing and future tax relief and programs to be effective and reach their target populations, several steps are required. First, the government must begin to shift the design of programs toward a social model of disability. It is essential as well to improve the knowledge base with respect to the needs of persons with disabilities. Productive two-way communication must also take place between the government and the disability community. We now turn our attention to these important areas.

Rethinking the Disability Tax Credit

Regardless of the specific route the government pursues in future, we believe that its work should be strongly influenced by a social model of disability. Even with our specific focus on disability tax measures, we found ourselves rethinking the conceptual base of these provisions. In fact, we tried to apply a social model of disability to one measure – the disability tax credit – that the Committee was asked to examine.

As noted in Chapter 1, a social model views disability largely as a problem of how well (or not) society accommodates impairment in function. When environments are adapted to individual need, a disability can change in severity or even disappear.

In our discussions of the disability tax credit, the past influence of the medical model became increasingly apparent. Eligibility is based on the *effects* of impairment on 'basic activities of daily living', which, at a general level, derives from the 'functional limitations' approach to disability that was current when the eligibility criteria were designed. However, the present criteria do not reflect accommodation of the person's disability except in a narrow medical context – taking into account how the effects can be mitigated by the use of appropriate devices, medication and therapy.

A social model of disability, on the other hand, recognizes that the impact of impairment is determined not only by the impaired function but also by other important individual and societal factors. A large body of research consistently documents the significance of these factors – e.g., how living circumstances can prolong a hospital stay, how environmental conditions can exacerbate a physical condition, and how family and community supports can substantially enhance recovery or the capacity to carry out activities of daily living.

Moreover, social models of disability do not discriminate against – or advantage – one type of impairment over another because they focus upon the restriction imposed not simply by the impairment alone but rather by the impairment within its context. For example, individuals who are blind are much less restricted in activities of daily living if they have ready access to information printed in Braille, traffic light standards with auditory walk signals and elevators with Braille panels than they would be without these resources. Persons with paraplegia might be far more mobile in an urban centre with ready access to para-transportation than in a remote community with few sidewalks and no accessible transportation.

The proposition that disability results from the interaction of three factors – human functions, daily activities and social context – is consistent with work under way throughout the world. In 2001, for example, the World Health Organization released the latest version of the International Classification of Functioning, Disability and Health, in which disability was seen to arise from the interaction between impairments and externally imposed limitations on activity.

In our view, if we were to apply a social model framework to the disability tax credit, the eligibility criteria could incorporate the following components: (i) an impairment in function, (ii) the effects of the impairment on the individual's activities, and (iii) biological, psychological, social and environmental factors necessary to assessing impairment in function and its impact on activity.

In our discussions, we recognized how practitioners might be confused by the inconsistent classification of functions and activities. As mentioned in Chapter 2, some 'activities' are really functions (e.g., seeing and eliminating) and some are really activities (e.g., dressing). We considered a broader list of functions for the disability tax credit that would reflect impairments in both mental and physical functions. These functions would include:

- neurological functions – diseases and conditions affecting the brain and spinal cord;

- mental functions – diseases and conditions affecting memory, problem solving, judgment, perception, learning, attention, concentration, verbal and non-verbal comprehension and expression, and the regulation of behaviour and emotions;

- motor functions – diseases and conditions affecting the movement and coordinated use of limbs;

- sensory functions – diseases and conditions affecting sight, hearing, taste, smell or touch;

- comprehension and expressive functions – diseases and conditions affecting the processing and production of language; and

- structure, organ and other physiological systems – diseases and conditions affecting bodily organs such as heart, lungs, liver, pancreas, bone and other structures, and endocrine and other regulatory systems.

Impairments in these functions then must result in a marked restriction in certain designated activities. In the case of a measure designed around a marked restriction in activities of daily living, such as the disability tax credit, the list of activities might include the following:

- self-care, such as eating, bathing or dressing;

- health and safety, such as managing necessary medications and risks to personal safety; and

- essential life management skills, such as paying bills, using public transportation, purchasing groceries, communicating and getting along with others.

It should be noted that the Committee discussed the use of the term 'basic' to modify activities of daily living for the purposes of the disability tax credit. While we did not recommend any changes to the *Income Tax Act* in this regard, the qualifier 'basic', in the view of some, can be considered unnecessarily limiting. This is why we decided not to use it in the context of our broader work on the conceptualization of disability.

No doubt, there would be debate around this list of activities of daily living. Some would argue, for example, that the list we developed in relation to the disability tax credit should include basic academic skills, such as reading and writing, or social skills such as getting along with others.

The identification of essential academic skills as an activity of daily living, for example, would help ensure the potential eligibility of persons with severe learning disabilities, who typically have difficulty qualifying for the disability tax credit. Others would argue that the inclusion of basic academic skills inadvertently would include persons who are illiterate or who may have difficulty reading the fine print of a newspaper.

Indeed, in our own deliberations regarding the disability tax credit in particular, we debated extensively the types of activities that should be considered 'activities of daily living' and their potential role in determining eligibility for the credit. It is clear that additional work would be required to identify possible indicators of marked restriction in activities of daily living.

One dimension in the development of such indicators involves the combination of type of activity and how much of the time the individual either cannot engage in the activity or requires an inordinate amount of time to engage in that activity. A qualified practitioner using specialized measures of assessment can determine clearly the *significance* of how an activity is performed. For example, certain behaviour may be slower than, less than or more present than a given norm.

Some activities might be restricted almost all the time but, depending on the circumstances, their restriction may be far less significant than an activity that is restricted some of the time. A person with Crohn's disease who spends an inordinate amount of time eliminating bodily waste three days a week, for instance, is arguably far more restricted than a person whose early stage neurological impairment makes it impossible for him or her to ride a bicycle.

We also noted in our discussions of the disability tax credit a number of concerns with the current use of the term 'all or substantially all' with respect to a marked restriction. Specifically, the term 'significant' could be viewed as fairer by persons with disabilities and it would be more meaningful to the health practitioners who certify the presence of marked restriction. However, the use of 'significant' could extend eligibility for the disability tax credit, at some fiscal cost.

We recognize that legislation is not necessarily framed in words that have a clear technical meaning to health practitioners or other specialists: the issue of how legislation should be drafted would have to be addressed. That being said, it would be helpful if the language used by the Canada Revenue Agency on its forms and explanatory material accords with the terminology normally used by health practitioners who complete the forms or deal with the material. Going forward, the Committee feels that the use of the term 'significant' in eligibility criteria for the disability tax credit might be given further consideration.

The Committee also acknowledges that a conceptualization of disability along these lines would create administrative challenges, particularly if applied within the tax system. Tax measures are blunt instruments that do not easily adjust for changes in personal capacity. The eligibility framework discussed above, by contrast, would be based on observations of individual behaviour within a set of social circumstances, and would be difficult to translate into criteria to be used for administering tax measures.

Despite the need for the further development of these ideas, we believe that our discussion of these issues puts in place a strong foundation for future work. It is a framework that takes into account the significance of context – which is continually evolving as new therapies, medications, assistive devices and other supports come on stream.

A social model of disability also helps ensure that the determination of disability keeps pace with changes in individual and social circumstances. While additional individuals may become eligible for various programs as their circumstances evolve, it is equally likely that others will go off these programs as their abilities are modified through the provision of supports, therapy or treatment. Perhaps the key dimension of a social model – the factor that distinguishes it from current tax measures and programs – is the recognition of the significant role of accommodation and its influence upon the real-life impact of the impairment. Marked restriction in activity is determined by the amount and effectiveness of accommodation in place in a given environment. Understanding and applying the concept of accommodation would move a long way toward putting into practice a social model of disability.

Knowledge Base

The federal government already has identified the development of the knowledge base on disability as a major objective. *Advancing the Inclusion of Persons with Disabilities 2002* pointed out that the development of policies to promote the inclusion of Canadians with disabilities requires knowledge of their current situations, the issues they face, and the successes and limitations of existing policy. The report notes that, in recent years, the limitations of current information have hampered progress in this area.[8]

The Committee supports selective investment in the collection and analysis of data that will help develop the knowledge base on disability. We were pleased that the 2004 federal budget included funding for the Participation and Activity Limitation Survey to be conducted in 2006.

The Committee suggests that the federal government build on this commitment by adding questions on disability, where feasible and appropriate, to new and existing surveys in order to improve the knowledge base in this area. Obtaining data through such surveys on a regular basis would provide a clearer picture of ongoing issues faced by persons with disabilities, including labour force attachment and changes in disability status over time.

Disability Tax Fairness

[8] Government of Canada, *Advancing the Inclusion of Persons with Disabilities*, 2002, p. 9.

Improved Communications

Throughout our deliberations, the Committee was struck by obvious weaknesses in the communication process between the members of the disability community and the government and its agencies. The processes for claiming eligibility for tax credits are generally not well understood. Many individuals whose application for the disability tax credit was denied did not know why their applications had been rejected and were not fully informed about the appeal process.

Shortcomings in the way in which information and concerns about programs are communicated are so serious as to imperil their proper and fair functioning. No matter how supportive the existing programs, Canadians will not be able to take full advantage of them unless they know of and understand these programs and their associated benefits.

Persons with disabilities need to be aware of the steps to claim eligibility for various measures, such as the disability tax credit. Improved access also requires that they have confidence in the fairness and openness of the way in which programs are administered.

The government, in turn, must create the means to receive input from the disability community and take every opportunity to involve it in decisions relating to the administration of existing programs and the design of new ones. There must be a strong, continued effort to improve communication if persons with disabilities are to receive equitable treatment.

For example, the Committee discussed whether, and under what conditions, family members or friends should be permitted to file income tax returns for persons with severe impairments in mental function. What makes this issue significant for persons with disabilities is the increasing importance of filing an income tax return in order to claim refundable credits or to document financial eligibility for benefits and services. It is to the advantage of virtually all low-income persons with disabilities to file an income tax and benefit return, even if they pay or owe no income tax for the year in question.

The Committee suggests that the Canada Revenue Agency emphasize in its communication strategy the importance to low-income persons with disabilities of filing tax returns. It is also essential to ensure that legal representatives are aware of their responsibility to file an income tax return on behalf of persons with disabilities who are not capable of doing so themselves.

We do note the positive signs of progress in the last two years. For example, the revisions to the T2201 form, which were introduced by the Canada Revenue Agency after extensive consultation with community groups and health practitioners, have resulted in a much-improved form. There is an urgent need to continue the progress achieved in recent years. We recommended in Chapter 2 on the disability tax credit that this consultation process continue and be applied to other areas as well.

The Committee has called for changes to legislation and forms to ensure clarity of interpretation and consistency with application of the disability tax credit. We have proposed various mechanisms for improved communication with respect to tax measures, from providing more information in Canada Revenue Agency publications to renaming the medical expense tax credit to indicate that it also recognizes disability-related expenses.

We have recommended the training of appropriate Canada Revenue Agency staff in all tax provisions related to persons with disabilities, and of qualified practitioners in eligibility issues relating to the disability tax credit, in particular. The Committee also recommended that the Canada Revenue Agency create an advisory committee to monitor the administration of various disability tax measures.

Persons with disabilities and their organizations have talked for many years about effective consultation mechanisms within government to ensure that disability issues are adequately addressed. At the national meeting in March 2004 on "Connecting People to Policy," the disability community identified the need for genuine engagement on policy issues. In their view, genuine engagement requires:

- broad representation of the disability community;
- resources for community participation;
- reporting to key decision makers (officials and politicians);
- the ability to look at issues from a cross-disability consumer perspective; and
- recognition of the need for horizontal (i.e., cross-departmental) collaboration.

The community has also proposed structures within government to respond to the range of concerns pertaining to disability. It has called for the appointment of a senior Minister responsible for disability issues across the Government of Canada. It sought – and achieved with the Office for Disability Issues – the creation of a coordinating body at a senior level with the capacity to engage in community and research issues. The disability community continues to press for the establishment of a grants and contributions program to enhance the capacity of disability organizations to participate in public policy debates.

Final Thoughts

We conclude this report with a few thoughts about the structure of our own Committee. Members of the Committee represented very diverse levels of knowledge and views on disability-related issues, and remarkably different backgrounds and experiences. While it was not easy to proceed from such a wide-ranging base, we believe that this diversity actually worked to our advantage.

Our Committee represented, in effect, the differing perceptions and views of Canadians on disability, on taxes and on government programs more generally. We knew that if we could reach consensus around some of the difficult issues with which we were grappling, we would have achieved an essential 'pre-testing' of ideas for the government. Our recommendations were subject to rigorous screening, given the diverse perspectives brought to the table.

We were clearly aided in our discussions by the rich legacy of work that other commissions and task forces have produced over the years. The Committee wishes to recognize, in particular, the value and the efforts of the House of Commons Standing Committee on Human Resources Development and the Status of Persons with Disabilities.

We support the continued need for such a committee of Parliament. As explained in the introductory chapter, we took explicit steps to build on the review of tax measures initiated by the parliamentary committee, using the submissions it had received and responding in this report to its numerous recommendations. We can only hope that our own work has made an equally valuable contribution to the lives of persons with disabilities and to Canadian society as a whole.

Summary of Recommendations

Summary of Recommendations

Chapter 2: Disability Tax Credit

RECOMMENDATION 2.1

The Committee recommends that:

> The *Income Tax Act* be amended to replace the present wording 'severe and prolonged mental or physical impairment' with the wording 'severe and prolonged impairment in physical or mental functions.'

This recommendation is for clarification purposes and does not involve any revenue cost. It is not intended to alter the scope of eligibility for the credit.

RECOMMENDATION 2.2

The Committee recommends that:

> The term 'perceiving, thinking and remembering' as a basic activity of daily living in the *Income Tax Act* and on the T2201 form, be replaced with the term 'mental functions necessary for everyday life.'
>
> In our view, mental functions are the range of processes that govern how people think, feel and behave. Based on our consultations and research, they include memory, problem solving, judgment, perception, learning, attention, concentration, verbal and non-verbal comprehension and expression, and the regulation of behaviour and emotions. These functions are necessary for activities of everyday life that are required for self-care, health and safety, social skills and simple transactions.

This recommendation is for clarification purposes and does not involve any revenue cost. It is not intended to alter the scope of eligibility for the credit.

RECOMMENDATION 2.3

The Committee recommends that:

> The Canada Revenue Agency state in its explanatory materials and on the application form for the disability tax credit that some impairments in function can result in a marked restriction in a basic activity of daily living, even though these impairments may have signs and symptoms that may be intermittent.

This action is not intended to alter the legislative requirement that a marked restriction in a basic activity of daily living be present 'all or substantially all of the time.' This recommendation should not involve any revenue cost.

RECOMMENDATION 2.4

The Committee recommends that:

The *Income Tax Act* be amended to provide that persons with a severe and prolonged impairment who are restricted in two or more basic activities of daily living qualify for the disability tax credit if the cumulative effects of the restriction are equivalent to a marked restriction in a single basic activity of daily living all or substantially all of the time.

This recommendation is estimated to involve a revenue cost of approximately $50 million annually.

RECOMMENDATION 2.5

The Committee recommends that:

The federal government ensure that the legislative and administrative requirements concerning the present interpretation regarding life-sustaining therapy adequately reflect the time taken for essential preparation, administration of and necessary recovery from life-sustaining therapy as recently interpreted in decisions of the Tax Court of Canada.

The revenue cost of this recommendation will ultimately depend on the nature of the changes implemented by the government.

RECOMMENDATION 2.6

The Committee recommends that:

The *Income Tax Act* be amended to include physiotherapists in the list of qualified practitioners eligible to certify for the purposes of the disability tax credit a marked restriction in walking.

The federal government consult with the Canadian Nurses Association to determine under what circumstances nurse practitioners could be allowed to certify eligibility for the disability tax credit.

This recommendation does not involve any revenue cost.

RECOMMENDATION 2.7

The Committee recommends that:

The Canada Revenue Agency:
- ensure that its staff follow the procedures relating to the disability tax credit in its Taxation Operations Manuals and Interpretation Bulletins;

- ensure that its general staff are able to assist persons with disabilities with respect to completing and filing the T2201 form, or refer them to appropriate specialized personnel where required;
- develop training programs, workshops and guidelines for its staff regarding changes to the legislation and interpretive guidelines for the disability tax credit, and the administration of tax measures for persons with disabilities;
- develop appropriate communications and educational material for qualified practitioners to assist them in completing the T2201 form;
- make clear in its communication materials that a second informal review is available to taxpayers denied the disability tax credit; and
- monitor the achievement of these recommendations.

Elements of this recommendation that are consistent with current practice do not involve any revenue cost. The Committee estimates that about $2 million annually will be required to implement the components of this recommendation that represent new initiatives.

RECOMMENDATION 2.8

The Committee recommends that:

The Canada Revenue Agency continue to improve the T2201 form by ensuring that:
- its ongoing consultations involve a wide representation of consumers and qualified practitioners regarding the T2201 form or related disability tax credit materials such as clarification letters and letters to individuals whose claim has been denied;
- the guidelines relating to the completion of the form are clear and concise to enable claimants and qualified practitioners to understand the eligibility criteria for the disability tax credit;
- examples and questions on the T2201 form reflect real-life situations to enable an appropriate determination of the severity of the impairment;
- examples and questions on the T2201 form continue to be revised as necessary and appropriate to reflect changes in legislation and court decisions; and
- data are collected, in order to evaluate the impact of the revisions to the T2201 form, on the number and percentage of successful and unsuccessful claims by basic activity of daily living, and claims for which additional information was requested (clarification letters) by basic activity of daily living.

This recommendation is largely consistent with current practice and would involve only minor costs.

RECOMMENDATION 2.9

The Committee recommends that:

> The Canada Revenue Agency take the following steps with respect to clarification letters:
>
> - specify in writing why clarification is required in order to help qualified practitioners address specific issues or concerns; and
> - ensure that all questions are relevant to the specific disability, instead of using a uniform approach for all impairments.

This recommendation does not involve any additional cost.

RECOMMENDATION 2.10

The Committee recommends that:

> The Canada Revenue Agency intensify its existing efforts to ensure that:
>
> - taxpayers who receive a letter denying their disability tax credit claims be:
>   (i) given specific reasons for the denial,
>   (ii) informed about their objection and appeal rights through a copy of the pamphlet, *Your Appeal Rights Under the Income Tax Act*, provided by the Agency,
>   (iii) informed that other persons, such as family members, friends or professional advisors, can act on their behalf, and
>   (iv) informed that they have access to documents in their file when the Canada Revenue Agency acknowledges receipt of the Notice of Objection through a copy of the pamphlet *Resolving your dispute – A more open, transparent process* provided by the Agency;
> - appeals officers have access, if required, to competent medical advice when reviewing Notice of Objection and additional medical reports; and
> - appeals officers meet with taxpayers or their representative in appropriate cases.

This recommendation should involve only minor incremental costs.

RECOMMENDATION 2.11

The Committee recommends that:

> The Canada Revenue Agency develop an alternative dispute resolution process for disability tax credit claims following an Appeals Branch denial, relying on an informal but independent process based on basic fairness criteria.

The Canada Revenue Agency mount a pilot project to test the operation of the suggested alternative dispute resolution process.

This pilot project is estimated to cost $4 million over one to two years. Ongoing costs would depend on the results of this pilot project.

RECOMMENDATION 2.12

The Committee recommends that:

In order to deal with the administrative aspects of the disability tax credit and the achievement of the previously enumerated recommendations, the Canada Revenue Agency form a consultative committee composed of consumer and professional representatives that would report directly to the Minister of National Revenue on all administrative aspects of the tax system related to persons with disabilities.

This recommendation should involve only minor costs.

RECOMMENDATION 2.13

The Committee recommends that:

The Canada Revenue Agency, in conjunction with the appropriate departments, undertake a review of Canada Pension Plan disability beneficiaries and disability tax credit claimants with the goal of evaluating possible reasons for the low take-up of the disability tax credit by CPP disability beneficiaries.

The Canada Revenue Agency work with other government departments to ensure that all applicants for CPP disability benefits are advised of their potential eligibility for the disability tax credit, and furnished with forms and information so that they can readily consider their eligibility and make an application for the disability tax credit if appropriate. If, as a result of this work, the government finds that there is a significant overlap in eligibility, it should explore whether a simplified application process or joint administration of some aspects of the two programs is warranted.

This recommendation has an unknown revenue cost. Additional tax relief offered through the disability tax credit arising from this recommendation should already be provided under existing legislation. This recommendation should involve only minor administrative costs.

Chapter 3: Employment- and Education-Related Tax Measures

RECOMMENDATION 3.1

To recognize the cost of required accommodation for persons with disabilities, the Committee recommended prior to the March 2004 federal budget that:

> **The government introduce a disability supports deduction to allow the full deductibility of the cost of disability supports purchased for the purposes of employment or education.**

The March 2004 budget implemented this proposal by introducing a disability supports deduction. The measure has an estimated cost of $15 million annually.

RECOMMENDATION 3.2

To further improve the disability supports deduction, the Committee recommends that:

> **The cost of such items as job coaches and readers, Braille note takers, page turners, print readers, voice-operated software, memory books, assistive devices used to access computer technology, and similar disability-related expenses be added to the list of expenses recognized by the deduction.**

We estimate that this improvement would cost $5 million annually.

RECOMMENDATION 3.3

The Committee recommends that:

> **The government change the name of the medical expense tax credit to the 'medical and disability expense tax credit.'**

There is no cost associated with this recommendation.

RECOMMENDATION 3.4

The Committee recommends that:

> **The Department of Finance and the Canada Revenue Agency review currently available data and, where possible, gather new data on the actual expenses being claimed under the medical expense tax credit, and consider the appropriateness of these claims.**

The estimated cost of this recommendation is nominal.

RECOMMENDATION 3.5

The Committee recommends that:

> The maximum credit under the refundable medical expense supplement be increased from $562 to $1,000 and continue to be indexed to the cost of living.

The estimated cost of this recommendation is $20 million per year.

RECOMMENDATION 3.6

To address the special needs of students with disabilities, the Committee recommends that:

> The time over which contributions may be made to a registered education savings plan for a person with a disability be extended to 25 years from 21 years, and that the time before the plans must be liquidated be extended from 25 to 30 years from inception.
>
> The government broaden the list of educational programs that qualify under registered education savings plans to ensure that they accommodate the more diverse needs of persons with disabilities.

The estimated cost of these measures is nominal.

RECOMMENDATION 3.7

The Committee recommends that:

> Information for businesses about the deductibility of capital expenses to accommodate persons with disabilities be made more widely available in Canada Revenue Agency guides.

The estimated cost of this recommendation is nominal.

RECOMMENDATION 3.8

The Committee recommends that:

> As part of its efforts to develop measures to encourage the full participation of persons with disabilities, the government review the effectiveness of the United States' Work Opportunity Tax Credit.

Chapter 4: Measures for Caregivers and Children with Disabilities

RECOMMENDATION 4.1

The Committee recommends that:

> The limit of expenses claimable under the medical expense tax credit by caregivers be increased from $5,000 to $10,000 for those with dependent relatives eligible for the disability tax credit.

The estimated cost of this measure is $5 million annually.

RECOMMENDATION 4.2

The Committee recommends that:

> The government review the RRSP/RRIF rules in order to allow additional flexibility in respect of a deceased's RRSP or RRIF proceeds left to a financially dependent child or grandchild with a disability. Such provisions should include allowing these proceeds to be rolled over to a discretionary trust for that individual, provided that no person other than the disabled beneficiary may access the income or capital of the trust during his or her lifetime.

The revenue cost of this measure is small.

RECOMMENDATION 4.3

The Committee recommends that:

> The federal government increase the amount of the Child Disability Benefit by $600 to raise the total maximum annual benefit from $1,653 to $2,253, and that this amount continue to be indexed to the cost of living.

The estimated cost of this measure is $15 million annually.

Chapter 5: Future Directions

RECOMMENDATION 5.1

Our previous recommendations represent priority actions to improve tax fairness for persons with disabilities. Going forward, the Committee recommends that:

> **Priority should be given to expenditure programs rather than tax measures to target new funding where the need is greatest. The Committee recognizes that the development of such programs would involve consultations with provincial and territorial governments and the disability community.**

Appendices

Appendix 1
List of Members[1,2]

Sherri Torjman (co-chair), Vice-President of the Caledon Institute of Social Policy, a national social policy research organization.

Robert Brown (co-chair), tax policy and economic consultant, a former Chair of Price Waterhouse and former Clifford Clark Visiting Economist – a key advisory position in the Department of Finance – from 1998 until 2001.

Brian J. Arnold, tax lawyer with Goodmans LLP and Professor Emeritus at the University of Western Ontario.

Michael Bach, Executive Vice-President of the Canadian Association for Community Living, a national advocacy organization for persons with intellectual disabilities.

Laurie Beachell, National Coordinator, Council of Canadians with Disabilities, a national advocacy association of persons with disabilities.

Harry Beatty, lawyer and consultant specializing in disability law and policy.

Gail Beck, M.D., C.M., F.R.C.P.C., Director, Youth Inpatient Psychiatry of the Royal Ottawa Hospital.

Gary Birch, Executive Director, Neil Squire Foundation, a national non-profit organization providing education, technology and career development for people with physical disabilities.

Lembi Buchanan, public relations consultant and Chair of the Coalition for Disability Tax Credit Reform.

Karen R. Cohen, Ph.D., C. Psych., Associate Executive Director and Registrar Accreditation, Canadian Psychological Association.

Yude M. Henteleff, C.M., Q.C., Senior Counsel to the Winnipeg law firm Pitblado and past President and current Honourary Solicitor of the Learning Disabilities Association of Canada.

Guy Lord, Senior Partner of the law firm Osler, Hoskin & Harcourt LLP.

---

[1] Dr. Claude A. Renaud, former Associate Secretary General and Chief Medical Officer with the Canadian Medical Association, was an original member of the Committee.

[2] Members represent themselves as individuals and not the organizations with which they are associated.

Appendix 2
List of Submissions

To the Sub-Committee of the House of Commons Standing Committee on Human Resources Development and the Status of Persons with Disabilities

Adèle Furrie Consulting Inc.
Alzheimer Society of Canada
ARCH: A Legal Resource Centre for Persons with Disabilities
Canadian Alliance on Mental Illness and Mental Health
Canadian Association for Community Living
Canadian Hard of Hearing Association
Canadian Medical Association
Canadian Mental Health Association
Canadian National Institute for the Blind
Canadian Psychiatric Association
Canadian Psychological Association
Confédération des organismes de personnes handicapées du Québec
Council of Canadians with Disabilities
Multiple Sclerosis Society of Canada
Learning Disabilities Association of Canada
Lembi Buchanan
Schizophrenia Society of Canada

To the Technical Advisory Committee on Tax Measures for Persons with Disabilities

Organizations

ARCH: A Legal Resource Centre for Persons with Disabilities
Autism Society of PEI
British Columbia Coalition of People with Disabilities
Canadian AIDS Society
Canadian Association of the Deaf
Canadian Association of Occupational Therapists
Canadian Association of Speech-Language Pathologists and Audiologists
Canadian Cystic Fibrosis Foundation
Canadian Diabetes Association
Canadian Hearing Society

Canadian Labour Congress
Canadian Life and Health Insurance Association Inc.
Canadian National Institute for the Blind
Canadian Paraplegic Association
Canadian Physiotherapy Association
Coalition for Disability Tax Credit (DTC) Reform
Diabetes Advocacy
Disability Services (University of Manitoba)
Epilepsy Canada
Mississauga Homes for Independent Living
Multiple Sclerosis Society of Canada
National Federation of the Blind
NWT Council of Persons with Disabilities
Office of the Commissioner of Review Tribunals (CPP/OAS)
Ontario Brain Injury Association
Opportunities through Rehabilitation and Work Society
Planned Lifetime Advocacy Network
Prince Edward Island Association for Community Living
Richmond Hill Fibromyalgia and Chronic Fatigue Syndrome Wellness Support Group
Schizophrenia Society of Canada
Voice for Hearing Impaired Children Ontario (Health Committee)

Individuals

Monique Beaudoin
Mark Bernier
Kelvin Blais
Carl Broughton
Angela Falkowska
Carolyn Forbes
Marla Hayes
Coleen Howey
Margaret Kraak
Anne Kramer
Penny Leclair
Rosemary Leslie
John Macdonald

Ellie McCaig
Lori Montcalm
Charlie Morgan
Lauri Morris
Kennedy O'Brien
Eileen Reppenhagen
Hans Rupprecht
Gord Shapley
Chris Stark
Libby Thaw
Beryl Williams
M. Kathleen Williams

Appendix 3
Research and Expert Consultation

In order to obtain background information and input for its review, the Committee undertook an extensive program of research and expert consultation on the important issues identified in its mandate. These activities, carried out in the initial year of the Committee's term, enabled us to benefit from work done by others in the field; new information, data and thoughts developed in the research process; and important input from experts and knowledgeable organizations.

We undertook the research process by commissioning studies on four major areas of interest. The research papers developed in this process focused upon economic principles and positive options for the reform of disability tax measures; the role of federal tax measures in advancing the inclusion of persons with disabilities in Canadian society; disability-related federal tax measures supporting education, training and employment; and tax issues with respect to Aboriginal Canadians with disabilities. The research papers were prepared by leading experts in their respective fields, most of whom then met with the Committee to discuss their reports and recommendations.

Officials from the Department of Finance and the Canada Revenue Agency were very helpful in providing relevant data and documentation requested by the Committee, and in supporting us in our work. Committee members themselves prepared discussion papers on a wide range of issues, including such topics as the design of new eligibility criteria for various tax provisions, the refundability of tax credits, administrative and communication issues relating to current tax provisions, the legal interpretation of terms, an overview of decisions arising from relevant court cases and dispute resolution procedures around current tax measures.

The Committee also consulted with selected experts when we felt it necessary to explore certain issues in more depth. We met, for example, with a professor from the University of Ottawa to review the distinction between 'physical and mental functions' and 'activities of daily living' in order to create a conceptually rigorous eligibility screen for the disability tax credit. The Committee also sought opinions from seven independent specialists in mental function on possible reforms of the disability tax credit.

An informal discussion was held with representatives from RBC Financial on their accommodation practices in hiring and retaining employees with disabilities. We also met with representatives from the Canadian Labour Congress to discuss various work-related tax provisions.

We consulted with a Montreal-based lawyer who specializes in mediation and alternative dispute resolution. Members of the Committee also met informally with representatives of a number of organizations representing different segments of the disability community to discuss issues and concerns, and to review alternative proposals for reform.

Finally, representatives of the Committee met in Quebec City with three researchers at Laval University who were carrying out a study on behalf of l'Office des personnes handicapées du Québec on disability-related income security programs and tax provisions. Two of these individuals subsequently made a presentation to our Committee.

The research and expert consultations carried out by the Committee provided the basis for discussions on the issues that we addressed. We are grateful for this invaluable support, and we hope that this work will provide not only a foundation for our recommendations in this report, but also a useful bank of information for further studies and consideration.

Appendix 4

Description of Federal Personal Income Tax Measures for Persons with Disabilities and Caregivers

Disability Tax Credit

The disability tax credit (DTC) provides tax relief to individuals who, due to the effects of a severe and prolonged mental or physical impairment, are markedly restricted in their ability to perform a basic activity of daily living as certified by a qualified health practitioner, or would be markedly restricted were it not for extensive therapy to sustain a vital function. Individuals are markedly restricted if, all or substantially all of the time, even with therapy or the use of appropriate devices and medication, they are blind or unable to perform a basic activity of daily living or require an inordinate amount of time to perform the activity. The basic activities of daily living are: walking; feeding or dressing oneself; perceiving, thinking and remembering; speaking; hearing; and eliminating bodily waste.

The DTC recognizes the impact of non-itemizable disability-related costs on an individual's ability to pay tax. For 2004, the credit is 16 percent of $6,486, which provides a federal tax reduction of up to $1,038. This credit can be transferred to a supporting spouse, parent, grandparent, child, grandchild, brother, sister, aunt, uncle, nephew or niece of the individual. The credit amount is fully indexed to inflation.

DTC Supplement for Children

Families caring for children with severe and prolonged impairments may receive additional tax relief through a supplement to the DTC. This additional tax relief was introduced in the 2000 budget. For 2004, the supplement provides an additional federal tax reduction of up to $605, or 16 percent of $3,784. The $3,784 supplement amount is reduced dollar-for-dollar by the amount of child care expenses or attendant care expenses claimed for tax purposes over $2,216. Both this income threshold and the supplement amount ($3,784) are fully indexed.

Medical Expense Tax Credit

The medical expense tax credit (METC) recognizes the effect of above-average disability-related and medical expenses on an individual's ability to pay tax. For 2004, the credit equals 16 percent of qualifying expenses in excess of the lesser of $1,813 and 3 percent of net income. The net income threshold is used to determine above-average expenses and it is fully indexed to inflation. There is no upper limit on the amount of eligible expenses that may be claimed.

The list of eligible disability-related and medical expenses is regularly reviewed and expanded in light of new technologies and other disability-specific or medically related items.

Taxpayers may claim the medical expenses that they or their spouses incur. The 2004 budget proposed to allow caregivers to claim more of the medical and disability-related expenses they incur on behalf of dependent relatives. Specifically, for medical expenses paid on behalf of dependent relatives, such as a grandparent, niece or nephew, taxpayers will be able to claim qualifying medical expenses that exceed the lesser of 3 percent of the dependant's net income and $1,813 (for 2004). The maximum eligible amount that can be claimed on behalf of dependent relatives will be $5,000.

Caregiver Credit

This credit was introduced in the 1998 budget to provide tax relief to individuals providing in-home care for a parent or grandparent 65 years of age or over, or an infirm dependent relative, including an adult child or grandchild, brother, sister, aunt, uncle, niece or nephew. For 2004, the maximum credit is $605 (16 percent of $3,784). The credit is reduced when the dependant's net income exceeds $12,921 and is fully phased out when the dependant's net income reaches $16,705.

The caregiver credit amount and the income threshold at which the credit starts to be reduced are fully indexed to inflation.

Infirm Dependant Credit

The infirm dependant credit provides tax relief to individuals providing support to an infirm relative who lives in a separate residence. More specifically, the infirm dependant credit may be claimed by taxpayers supporting a child or grandchild 18 years of age or over, parent, grandparent, brother, sister, aunt, uncle, niece, or nephew, who is dependent due to a mental or physical infirmity. This non-refundable credit has a maximum value of $605 (16 percent of $3,784). The credit can be claimed by a supporting relative when the net income of the dependant is less than $9,152. The credit is reduced when the dependant's net income exceeds $5,368. This credit amount and the income threshold at which the credit starts to be reduced are fully indexed to inflation.

Disability Supports Deduction

The 2004 budget proposed to replace the attendant care deduction with a broader disability supports deduction that will allow expenses in respect of disability supports (e.g., sign language interpreters and talking textbooks) to be deducted from income if they are incurred for education or employment purposes. As a result, income used to pay for these expenses will not be taxed and will not affect income-tested benefits.

In the case of an employee, the deduction will generally be limited to the lesser of the amounts paid for eligible expenses and the taxpayer's earned income. A similar limit also applies to students, except that they can claim the deduction against non-earned income, subject to the length of their education program.

The list of expenses eligible for this deduction is specified. The need for some of these supports has to be certified by a medical practitioner.

Individuals need not be eligible for the disability tax credit in order to claim expenses under the disability supports deduction.

Expenses claimed under the disability supports deduction will not be claimable under the medical expense tax credit. Persons who purchase disability supports for purposes other than education or employment will still be able to claim them under the medical expense tax credit.

Other Personal Income Tax Measures

Persons with disabilities or those who care for them benefit from a number of special enhancements to other tax measures.

Home Buyers' Plan

Persons with disabilities or their relatives may withdraw up to $20,000 from a registered retirement savings plan (RRSP) on a tax-free basis to buy a home that is more accessible for, or better suited for the care of, an individual with a disability, even if the purchaser is not a first-time home buyer. Amounts withdrawn under the Home Buyers' Plan are required to be repaid to the individual's RRSP over a period of 15 years.

RRSP/RRIF Rollovers for an Infirm Child

When the annuitant under a RRSP or registered retirement income fund (RRIF) dies, the existing income tax rules generally provide that the value of the RRSP or RRIF is included in computing the deceased's income for the year of death. However, preferential tax treatment on RRSP or RRIF distributions made after death is provided in certain cases, including where the proceeds are distributed to a child or grandchild who was financially dependent on the deceased annuitant by reason of physical or mental infirmity. In this case, the RRSP or RRIF proceeds may be transferred without tax to the RRSP of the child or may be used to purchase an immediate life annuity.

For 2004, a child or grandchild is considered to be financially dependent if the child's income for the year preceding the year of death was below $14,035 (this threshold is indexed to inflation). A child with income above this amount may also be considered to be financially dependent, but only if the dependency can be demonstrated based on the particular facts of the situation.

Education Amount

Students with disabilities can claim the full-time education amount ($400 per month) for each month of part-time study at a post-secondary institution or occupational training program certified by the Minister of Human Resources and Skills Development. Eligible students include those who qualify for the DTC and those who cannot reasonably be expected to be enrolled as a full-time student because of a certified mental or physical impairment. In order to meet the part-time requirement, the student's program must be at least three weeks long and involve at least 12 hours of coursework per month.

Registered Education Savings Plans

Generally, a student has to be registered full time at a qualifying post-secondary institution in order to receive a payment out of a registered education savings plan (RESP) to further his/her post-secondary education. The full-time requirement is waived for students who qualify for the DTC and those who cannot reasonably be expected to be enrolled as a full-time student because of a certified mental or physical impairment.

Lifelong Learning Plans

Under the Lifelong Learning Plan (LLP), participants can access up to $10,000 in a calendar year, and up to a maximum of $20,000, from their registered retirement savings plans (RRSPs). Withdrawals can be made over four consecutive years. These funds are not subject to tax upon withdrawal, as would usually be the case for RRSP withdrawals, and remain untaxed as long as they are repaid to the RRSP over a period of no more than 10 years after the conclusion of studies.

In general, this provision applies only to full-time students. However, persons with disabilities are often unable to attend a post-secondary institution on a full-time basis because of their disability. Consequently, students who qualify for the DTC and those who cannot reasonably be expected to be enrolled as a full-time student because of a certified mental or physical impairment can be enrolled on a part-time basis and participate in the LLP. The program in which the student is enrolled must still be a qualifying educational program that normally requires a student to spend 10 hours or more per week on courses or work in the program.

Child Care Expense Deduction

The child care expense deduction (CCED) recognizes the child care costs incurred by single parents and two-earner families in the course of earning business or employment income, pursuing education or performing research. The child care costs of couples may also be recognized when one or both parents are pursuing education, or when one parent is incapable of caring for children due to a mental or physical infirmity. The infirmity needs to be certified in writing by a medical doctor.

The CCED limit is more generous in respect of children who qualify for the DTC ($10,000), and DTC-eligible children are considered eligible for the purposes of the CCED at any age. For children who do not qualify for the DTC, the limit is $7,000 for children under 7 years of age and $4,000 for other children.

Benefits delivered through the tax system

Refundable Medical Expense Supplement

The supplement improves work incentives for Canadians with disabilities and others with above-average medical expenses by helping to offset the loss of disability-related support when they enter the paid labour force. It provides assistance for above-average disability and medical expenses to low-income working Canadians. For 2004, the maximum supplement is the lesser of $562 and 25 percent of the medical expense tax credit and the disability supports deduction claims. The credit is available to workers with earnings above $2,809. To target assistance to those with low incomes, the credit is reduced by five percent of family income in excess of $21,301. Individuals claiming the refundable supplement may also claim the non-refundable medical expense tax credit and/or the disability supports deduction. This supplement was introduced in the 1997 budget and is fully indexed to inflation.

Child Disability Benefit

In recognition of the special needs of low- and modest-income families with a child with a disability, the 2003 budget introduced the Child Disability Benefit (CDB). The CDB is a supplement of the Canada Child Tax Benefit (CCTB), and is paid for children who meet the eligibility criteria for the DTC. For the July 2004 to June 2005 benefit year, eligible recipients receive their annual CDB entitlement of up to $1,653 per qualified child as part of their monthly CCTB issuance.

The full $1,653 Child Disability Benefit is provided for each eligible child to families with net income below the amount at which the National Child Benefit (NCB) supplement is fully phased out ($35,000 in July 2004 for families having three or fewer children). Beyond that income level, the CDB is reduced based on family income at the same rates as the NCB supplement. For the 2004-2005 benefit year, benefits are reduced by 12.2 percent for one disabled child, 22.7 percent for two disabled children and 32.5 percent for three or more disabled children. Accordingly, the CDB will be reduced to zero as net family income reaches $48,549 for a family caring for one disabled child, $49,564 for a family caring for two disabled children and $50,258 for a family caring for three disabled children. The CDB amount and income thresholds are indexed to inflation.

Appendix 5

The Disability Tax Credit and Horizontal Equity

Assume there are two individuals: Paul who has a severe disability, and Anne who does not. Both Paul and Anne have a total income of $25,000. However, due to his disability, Paul incurs non-itemizable expenses of $6,486, leaving him with less disposable income than Anne.

The principle of horizontal equity would suggest that because Paul incurs non-itemizable disability-related expenses that Anne does not, Paul should pay less tax than Anne. If there were no disability tax credit, this principle would be violated, since Paul would pay the same amount of federal tax as Anne. With the disability tax credit, Paul is able to receive tax relief for the non-itemizable disability-related expenses he incurs, lowering his tax bill relative to Anne's. Thus, in this example, horizontal equity is achieved.

How the Disability Tax Credit (DTC) Works

	Anne	Paul (no DTC)	Paul (with DTC)
Total income (A)	$25,000	$25,000	$25,000
Gross federal tax payable (16% of A)	4,000	4,000	4,000
Less: basic personal credit (16% of $8,012)	1,282	1,282	1,282
Less: DTC (16% of $6,486)			1,038
Basic federal tax (B)	$2,718	$2,718	$1,680
After-tax income (A-B)	$22,282	$22,282	$23,320

It should be noted that, in this example, horizontal equity is achieved only for individuals who pay tax at the lowest tax rate (i.e., who have incomes up to $35,000 in 2004). This situation arises because the tax relief offered by the disability tax credit is delivered as a non-refundable credit rather than a deduction. A credit ensures the same amount of tax relief regardless of income while a deduction, by contrast, affords greater tax relief for those with higher incomes.

Appendix 6
T2201, Disability Tax Credit Certificate

Canada Customs and Revenue Agency   Agence des douanes et du revenu du Canada

DISABILITY TAX CREDIT CERTIFICATE

Applicants: Read this page for information on the disability amount. See page 2 for instructions on how to apply.

Qualified persons: Read this page for information on the disability amount. See page 3 for instructions on completing Part B.

If you have a mental or physical impairment that is **severe** and **prolonged**, use this certificate for the following tax purposes:

- to determine if you can claim the disability amount (or to support related claims). The disability amount is a non-refundable tax credit used to reduce income tax payable on your return. This amount includes a supplement for persons under 18 at the end of the year. All or part of this amount may be transferred to your spouse or common-law partner, or another supporting person. For details on the disability amount, visit our Web site at **www.ccra.gc.ca/disability**, or see guide RC4064, *Information Concerning People With Disabilities*.

- to determine eligibility for the **Child Disability Benefit**, an amount available under the Canada Child Tax Benefit for a child with a disability under 18. For details, visit our Web site at **www.ccra.gc.ca/benefits** or see pamphlet T4114, *Your Canada Child Tax Benefit.*

If we have already determined that you are eligible, do not send another form unless the previous period of approval has ended, or we ask you to send in a new form. In the meantime, you must tell us if your condition improves.

When are you eligible?

A **qualified person** must certify on this form that you have a **prolonged** impairment, and that the effects of the impairment are such that one of the following applies (see definitions on this page):

- You are blind, even with the use of corrective lenses or medication.
- You are **markedly restricted** in any of the following basic acitivities of daily living:

  - walking
  - speaking
  - hearing
  - dressing
  - feeding
  - elimination (bowel or bladder functions)
  - perceiving, thinking, and remembering

- You need, and must dedicate a certain amount of time specifically for, **life-sustaining therapy**.

If you receive Canada Pension Plan or Quebec Pension Plan disability benefits, workers' compensation benefits, or other types of disability or insurance benefits, **it does not necessarily mean you are eligible for the disability amount**. These programs have other purposes and different criteria, such as an individual's inability to work.

The Canada Customs and Revenue Agency must validate this certificate for you to be eligible for either the disability amount or the Child Disability Benefit.

Definitions

Qualified person – Qualified persons are medical doctors, optometrists, audiologists, occupational therapists, psychologists, and speech-language pathologists. The table on page 2 lists which sections of the form each can certify.

Prolonged – An impairment is prolonged if it has lasted, or is expected to last, for a continuous period of at least 12 months.

Markedly restricted – You are markedly restricted if, all or substantially all the time, you are unable (or it takes you an inordinate amount of time) to perform a basic activity of daily living, even with therapy (other than life-sustaining therapy) and the use of appropriate devices and medication.

Life-sustaining therapy – Life-sustaining therapy is therapy you need to support a vital function. You must also need to dedicate time specifically for this therapy—at least three times per week, for an average of at least 14 hours per week. Examples of life-sustaining therapy include chest physiotherapy to help in breathing, or kidney dialysis to filter your blood. It **does not** include implanted devices such as a pacemaker, or special programs of diet, exercise, hygiene, or medication. Eligibility under this criterion applies only to 2000 and later years.

Note: You are responsible for any fees that the qualified person charges to complete this form or to give us more information. However, you may be able to claim these fees as medical expenses on line 330 of your tax return. See your tax guide for details.

If you want more information or need to contact us, call **1-800-959-8281**.

Visually impaired persons can get this form in braille, large print, or etext (computer diskette), or on audio cassette by visiting our Web site at **www.ccra.gc.ca/alternate** or by calling **1-800-267-1267** weekdays from 8:15 a.m. to 5:00 p.m. (Eastern Time).

Part A – To be completed by the person with the disability (or a representative)

Step 1: Complete this page (**please print**). Remember to sign the authorization area below.

Step 2: Take this form to a qualified person (use the table at right to find out who can certify the section(s) that applies).

Step 3: Send the completed form to one of the offices listed at the bottom of this page.
Keep a copy for your records.

When reviewing your claim, we may contact you or a qualified person (named on this certificate or attached document) who knows about your impairment, if we need more information.

Qualified person	Can certify:
Medical doctors	**all** sections (pages 3 - 7)
Optometrists	vision
Audiologists	hearing
Occupational therapists	walking; feeding; dressing
Psychologists	perceiving, thinking, and remembering
Speech-language pathologists	speaking

Information about the person with the disability

First name and initial　　　　　Last name　　　　　　　Maiden name (if applicable)　　Male　Female
☐　☐

Address:
Apt. No. – Street No. and name　　　　　　　　　　　　　　　Social insurance number

P.O. Box, R.R.

City　　　　　　　　　　　　　Prov./Terr.　Postal code　　　Date of birth
　　　　　　　　　　　　　　　　　　　　　　　　　　　　Year　Month　Day

Information about the applicant (if different from above)

First name and initial　　　　　Last name　　　　　　　Social insurance number

The person with the disability is:　☐ my spouse or common-law partner　☐ other (specify)

Does the person with the disability live with you? . . . . **yes** ☐　**no** ☐

If *no*, does the person with the disability depend on you for one or more of the basic necessities of life (such as food, shelter, or clothing)? . . . . **yes** ☐　**no** ☐

If *yes*, provide details:

If you need more space, attach a separate sheet of paper.

Authorization

As the person with the disability or their representative, I authorize the qualified person(s) having relevant clinical records, to provide the information contained in those records on or with this certificate, to the Canada Customs and Revenue Agency for the purpose of determining eligibility.

Sign here　　　　　　　　　　　　　　Telephone (　　)　　　　　　　Date

St. John's Tax Centre
PO Box 12071 Stn A
St. John's NL A1B 3Z1

International Tax Services Office
2204 Walkley Road
Ottawa ON K1A 1A8

Sudbury Tax Services Office
PO Box 20000 Stn A
Sudbury ON P3A 5C1

Winnipeg Tax Centre
PO Box 14000 Stn Main
Winnipeg MB R3C 3M2

Summerside Tax Centre
102-275 Pope Road
Summerside PE C1N 5Z7

Shawinigan-Sud Tax Centre
PO Box 3000 Stn Main
Shawinigan-Sud QC G9N 7S6

Jonquière Tax Centre
PO Box 1900 Stn LCD
Jonquière QC G7S 5J1

Surrey Tax Centre
9755 King George Highway
Surrey BC V3T 5E1

Part B – To be completed by qualified persons (see chart on page 2)

You must assess the following two criteria of your patient's impairment **separately**:

- **Effects** of the impairment – they must be such that the patient is blind, markedly restricted, or needs life-sustaining therapy (as described on pages 3 to 7). Eligibility is based on the effects of your patient's impairment in addition to the presence of that impairment.

- **Duration** of the impairment – the impairment must be prolonged (it must have lasted, or be expected to last, for a continuous period of at least 12 months).

Step 1: Answer the questions in the section(s) on pages 3 to 7 that apply to your patient (refer to the table at right).

Section	Page
Vision	Page 3
Walking	Page 4
Speaking	Page 4
Hearing	Page 5
Dressing	Page 5
Feeding	Page 6
Elimination (bowel or bladder functions)	Page 6
Perceiving, thinking, and remembering	Page 7
Life-sustaining therapy	Page 7

> **Note:**
> Whether completing this form for a child or an adult, assess your patient relative to someone of a similar chronological age who does not have the marked restriction.

Step 2: Complete the **"Effects of impairment," "Duration,"** and **"Certification"** sections on page 8.

Not applicable ☐

Vision

Your patient is considered **blind** if, all or substantially all the time, even with the use of corrective lenses or medication:

- visual acuity in **both** eyes is 20/200 (6/60) or less with the Snellen Chart (or an equivalent); or
- the greatest diameter of the field of vision in **both** eyes is 20 degrees or less.

Is your patient **blind**, as described above? .... yes ☐ no ☐

If *yes*, when did your patient's blindness begin? .... Year ☐☐☐☐

	Right eye	Left eye
What is your patient's visual acuity **after correction**?		
What is your patient's visual field **after correction** (in degrees if possible)?		

Part B – (continued)

Walking

Not applicable ☐

Your patient is considered **markedly restricted** in walking if, all or substantially all the time, he or she:

- is **unable** to walk even with appropriate therapy, medication, and devices; or
- requires an **inordinate amount of time** to walk, even with appropriate therapy, medication, and devices.

   Notes:
   - Devices for walking include canes, walkers, etc.
   - An **inordinate amount of time** means that walking takes **significantly** longer than for an average person who does not have the impairment.

Examples of markedly restricted in walking (examples are not exhaustive):

- Your patient must always rely on a wheelchair, even for short distances outside of his home.
- Your patient can walk 100 metres (or approximately one city block), but only by taking a significant amount of time, stopping because of shortness of breath or because of pain, all or substantially all the time.

Is your patient **markedly restricted** in walking, as described above? . . . . **yes** ☐ **no** ☐

If *yes*, when did your patient's marked restriction in walking begin? . . . . Year ☐☐☐☐

Speaking

Not applicable ☐

Your patient is considered **markedly restricted** in speaking if, all or substantially all the time, he or she:

- is **unable** to speak so as to be understood by another person familiar with the patient, in a quiet setting, even with appropriate therapy, medication, and devices; or
- takes an **inordinate amount of time** to speak so as to be understood by a person familiar with the patient, in a quiet setting, even with appropriate therapy, medication, and devices.

   Notes:
   - Devices for speaking include tracheoesophageal prostheses, vocal amplification devices, etc.
   - An **inordinate amount of time** means that speaking so as to be understood takes **significantly** longer than for an average person who does not have the impairment.

Examples of markedly restricted in speaking (examples are not exhaustive):

- Your patient must rely on other means of communication, such as sign language or a symbol board, all or substantially all the time.
- In your office, you must ask your patient to repeat words and sentences several times, and it takes a significant amount of time for her to make herself understood.

Is your patient **markedly restricted** in speaking, as described above? . . . . **yes** ☐ **no** ☐

If *yes*, when did your patient's marked restriction in speaking begin? . . . . Year ☐☐☐☐

Hearing

Not applicable ☐

Your patient is considered **markedly restricted** in hearing if, all or substantially all the time, he or she:

- is **unable** to hear so as to understand another person familiar with the patient, in a quiet setting, even with the use of appropriate devices; or

- takes an **inordinate amount of time** to hear so as to understand another person familiar with the patient, in a quiet setting, even with the use of appropriate devices.

  Notes:
  - Devices for hearing include hearing aids, cochlear implants, etc.
  - An **inordinate amount of time** means that hearing so as to understand takes **significantly** longer than for an average person who does not have the impairment.

Examples of markedly restricted in hearing (examples are not exhaustive):

- Your patient must rely completely on lip reading or sign language, despite using a hearing aid, in order to understand a spoken conversation, all or substantially all the time.
- In your office, you must raise your voice and repeat words and sentences several times, and it takes a significant amount of time for your patient to understand you, despite using a hearing aid.

Is your patient **markedly restricted** in hearing, as described above?.................................... yes ☐ no ☐

If *yes*, when did your patient's marked restriction in hearing begin? .... | Year | | |

Dressing

Not applicable ☐

Your patient is considered **markedly restricted** in dressing if, all or substantially all the time, he or she:

- is **unable** to dress himself or herself, even with appropriate therapy, medication, and devices; or

- requires an **inordinate amount of time** to dress himself or herself, even with appropriate therapy, medication, and devices.

  Notes:
  - Dressing oneself **does not** include identifying, finding, and shopping for or otherwise procuring clothing.
  - Devices for dressing include specialized buttonhooks, long-handled shoehorns, grab rails, safety pulls, etc.
  - An **inordinate amount of time** means that dressing takes **significantly** longer than for an average person who does not have the impairment.

Examples of markedly restricted in dressing (examples are not exhaustive):

- Your patient cannot dress without daily assistance from another person.
- Due to pain, stiffness, and decreased dexterity, your patient requires an inordinate amount of time to dress on a daily basis.

Is your patient **markedly restricted** in dressing, as described above?.................................... yes ☐ no ☐

If *yes*, when did your patient's marked restriction in dressing begin? .... | Year | | |

Part B – (continued)

Feeding

Your patient is considered **markedly restricted** in feeding if, all or substantially all the time, he or she:

- is **unable** to feed himself or herself, even with appropriate therapy, medication, and devices; or

- requires an **inordinate amount of time** to feed himself or herself, even with appropriate therapy, medication, and devices.

   Notes:
   - Feeding oneself **does not** include identifying, finding, shopping for or otherwise procuring food.
   - Feeding oneself **does** include preparing food, **except** when the time associated is related to a dietary restriction or regime.
   - Devices for feeding include modified utensils, etc.
   - An **inordinate amount of time** means that feeding takes **significantly** longer than for an average person who does not have the impairment.

Examples of markedly restricted in feeding (examples are not exhaustive):
- Your patient requires tube feedings, all or substantially all the time, for nutritional sustenance.
- Your patient requires an inordinate amount of time to prepare meals or to feed herself, on a daily basis, due to significant pain and decreased strength and dexterity in her upper limbs.

Is your patient **markedly restricted** in feeding, as described above?.............................. **yes** ☐ **no** ☐

If *yes*, when did your patient's marked restriction in feeding begin? .... Year ☐☐☐☐

Elimination (bowel or bladder functions)

Your patient is considered **markedly restricted** in elimination if, all or substantially all the time, he or she:

- is **unable** to personally manage bowel or bladder functions, even with appropriate therapy, medication, and devices; or

- requires an **inordinate amount of time** to personally manage bowel or bladder functions, even with appropriate therapy, medication, and devices.

   Notes:
   - Devices for elimination include catheters, ostomy appliances, etc.
   - An **inordinate amount of time** means that personally managing elimination takes **significantly** longer than for an average person who does not have the impairment.

Examples of markedly restricted in elimination (examples are not exhaustive):
- Your patient needs the assistance of another person to empty and tend to his colostomy appliance on a daily basis.
- Your patient is incontinent of bladder functions, all or substantially all the time, and requires an inordinate amount of time to manage and tend to her incontinence pads on a daily basis.

Is your patient **markedly restricted** in elimination, as described above?.............................. **yes** ☐ **no** ☐

If *yes*, when did your patient's marked restriction in elimination begin? .... Year ☐☐☐☐

Part B – (continued)

Perceiving, thinking, and remembering

Your patient is considered **markedly restricted** in perceiving, thinking, and remembering if, all or substantially all the time, he or she:

- is **unable** to perform the mental functions necessary for everyday life, by himself or herself, even with appropriate therapy, medication, and devices; or

- requires an **inordinate amount of time** to perform the mental functions necessary for everyday life, by himself or herself, even with appropriate therapy, medication, and devices.

Notes:

- Mental functions necessary for everyday life include:
  - Memory (for example, the ability to remember simple instructions, basic personal information such as name and address, or material of importance and interest);
  - Problem-solving, goal-setting, and judgement (for example, the ability to solve problems, set and keep goals, and make appropriate decisions and judgements); and
  - Adaptive functioning (for example, abilities related to self-care, health and safety, social skills and common, simple transactions).
- Devices for perceiving, thinking, and remembering include memory aids, adaptive aids, etc.
- An **inordinate amount of time** means that perceiving, thinking, and remembering takes **significantly** longer than for an average person who does not have the impairment.

Examples of markedly restricted in perceiving, thinking, and remembering (examples are not exhaustive):

- Your patient is unable to leave the house, all or substantially all the time, due to anxiety, despite medication and therapy.
- Your patient is independent in some aspects of everyday living; however, despite medication and therapy, needs daily support and supervision due to an inability to accurately interpret her environment.
- Your patient is incapable of making a common, simple transaction without assistance, all or substantially all the time.
- Your four-year-old patient cannot play interactively with his peers or understand simple requests .

Is your patient **markedly restricted** in perceiving, thinking, and remembering? . . . . **yes** ☐ **no** ☐

If *yes*, when did your patient's marked restriction in perceiving, thinking, and remembering begin? . . . . | Year | | | |

Life-sustaining therapy (applies to 2000 and later years)

Your patient must need life-sustaining therapy to support a vital function, even if the therapy has alleviated the symptoms. Examples of life-sustaining therapy are chest physiotherapy to facilitate breathing and kidney dialysis to filter blood. However, implanted devices such as a pacemaker, or special programs of diet, exercise, hygiene, or medication **do not** qualify.

Your patient must specifically dedicate the time needed for this therapy—at least three times per week, for an average of at least 14 hours per week (**do not** include time needed for travel, medical appointments, or to recuperate after therapy).

Does your patient meet the conditions for **life-sustaining therapy**, as described above? . . . . **yes** ☐ **no** ☐

If *yes*, answer the following two questions:

When did your patient's need for life-sustaining therapy begin? . . . . | Year | | | |

Specify the type of therapy: _____

Part B – (continued: complete all areas below)

Effects of impairment

Describe the effects of your patient's impairment on his or her ability to perform a basic activity of daily living.
If you need more space below, attach a separate sheet of paper.

Notes:
- Effects must be those which, even with therapy and the use of appropriate devices and medication, cause your patient to be markedly restricted **all or substantially all of the time**.
- Basic activities of daily living are limited to: walking; speaking; hearing; dressing; feeding; elimination; and perceiving, thinking, and remembering.
- Working, housekeeping, and social or recreational activities are **not** considered basic activities of daily living.
- This section may not be relevant for patients who are blind or in need of life-sustaining therapy.

Examples of effects of impairment (examples are not exhaustive):
- For a patient with a walking impairment, you might state the number of hours spent in bed or in a wheelchair each day.
- For a patient with an impairment in perceiving, thinking, and remembering, you might describe the degree to which your patient needs support and supervision.

_____
_____
_____
_____
_____
_____
_____

Diagnosis (if available): _____
_____

Duration

Has your patient's impairment lasted, or is it expected to last, for a continuous period of at least 12 months? .... yes ☐ no ☐

If *yes*, has the impairment improved, or is it likely to improve, such that the patient would no longer be markedly restricted, blind, or in need of life-sustaining therapy?.............. yes ☐ no ☐ unsure ☐

If *yes*, state the year that the improvement occured, or may be expected to occur .... ☐☐☐☐

Certification

Check whichever of the following applies to you:

☐ Medical doctor ☐ Optometrist ☐ Audiologist ☐ Occupational therapist ☐ Psychologist ☐ Speech-language pathologist

As a **qualified person**, I certify that to the best of my knowledge the information given in Part B is correct and complete.

Sign here

_____

Print your name

_____

Date

_____

Telephone
( )

Address

Note: If further information or clarification is needed, the CCRA may contact you.

Appendix 7

Departmental and Agency Staff and Others Assisting in the Preparation of the Report

Committee Secretary:

Charles Smyth, Department of Finance

Department of Finance and Canada Revenue Agency Ex-officio Participants on the Committee:

Chris Forbes, Department of Finance

Maureen Tapp, Canada Revenue Agency

Research Staff:

Annik Bordeleau, Department of Finance

Christopher Camp, Consultant

Galen Countryman, Department of Finance

Pierre LeBlanc, Department of Finance

Glenda Stark, Canada Revenue Agency

Hope Walton, Canada Revenue Agency

Administrative Staff:

Christine Hamel, Department of Finance

Marika Stamos, Canada Revenue Agency

Editors:

Maurice Michaud, NéoScript enr., Gatineau

Judith Richer of the **gordon**group, Ottawa

Translation:

Société Gamma Inc., Ottawa

Graphic Design:

Ryan/Smith Design Associates Inc., Ottawa

Bibliography

Bibliography

Blais, Gardner and Lareau, *Un système de compensation plus équitable pour les personnes handicapées*, Office des personnes handicapées du Québec, 2004.

Crawford, Cameron, *Federal Tax Measures and the Employment, Education and Training of People with Disabilities*, 2003.

Decima Research Inc., *National Profile of Family Caregivers in Canada – 2002*, 2002.

Department of Finance Canada, *Tax Expenditures and Evaluations: 2004*, 2004.

Department of Finance Canada, *The Budget Plan 2004*, 2004.

Federal Task Force on Disability Issues, *Equal Citizenship for Canadians with Disabilities: The will to act*, 1996.

Government of Canada, *Advancing the Inclusion of Persons with Disabilities*, 2002.

Government of Canada, *Defining Disability: A Complex Issue*, 2003.

Government of Canada, *Response to "Listening to Canadians: A First View of the Future of the Canada Pension Plan Disability Program,"* 2003.

House of Commons Standing Committee on Human Resources Development and the Status of Persons with Disabilities, *Getting It Right for Canadians: The Disability Tax Credit*, 2002.

House of Commons Standing Committee on Human Resources Development and the Status of Persons with Disabilities, *Listening to Canadians: A First View of the Future of the Canada Pension Plan Disability Program*, 2003.

House of Commons Standing Committee on Human Resources Development and the Status of Persons with Disabilities, *Tax Fairness for Persons with Disabilities*, 2002.

Human Resources Development Canada, *Disability in Canada: A 2001 Profile*, 2003.

Organisation for Economic Co-operation and Development, *Human Capital Investment: An International Comparison*, 1998.

Prince, Michael J., *People with Disabilities and Taxation in Canada: The Role of Federal Tax Measures in Advancing Inclusion and Full Citizenship*, 2003.

Roeher Institute, *Moving In Unison into Action: Towards a Policy Strategy for Improving Access to Disability Supports*, 2002.

Smart, Michael, and Mark Stabile, *Tax Support for the Disabled in Canada*, 2003.

Statistics Canada, General Social Survey, *Cycle 16: Caring for an aging society*, Catalogue no. 89-582-XIE, 2003.

Statistics Canada, Participation and Activity Limitation Survey, 2001, *Children with disabilities and their families*, Catalogue no. 89-585-XIE, 2003.

Statistics Canada, Participation and Activity Limitation Survey, 2001, *Disability Supports in Canada, 2001 – Tables*, Catalogue no. 89-581-XIE, 2003.

Statistics Canada, *Projected Population, By Age Group and Sex, Canada, Provinces and Territories, July 1, 2000–2026, Annual (Persons)*, CANSIM table 052-0001, 2004.

Valentine, Fraser, *Exploring the Relationship Between the Tax System and Aboriginal Peoples with Disabilities*, 2003.